The

# Four-letter Word

# The
# INVISIBLE
# Four-letter Word

## The secret to getting what you really want in life

## SCOTT A. SHUMWAY

ISBN
979-8-9865923-0-5
Paperback Edition – Nov 14, 2023

Content consulting, editing, and desktop publishing by Lisa Burt
Psychology research consulting by Brock Bumgarner
Cover design by Scott Shumway
Pyramid and Core graphics design by PresentationGO.com

For additional resources, training materials, and online tools about *The Invisible Four-letter Word*, visit invisiblefourletterword.com.
To inquire about a possible speaking engagement or for specialized training,
visit emiment.com, email us at info@emiment.com, or call us at 309-emiment (309-364-6368).

*Dedicated to Michael*

# TABLE OF CONTENTS

## Section One — The Problem

## Section Two — The Solution

## Section Three — The Application

# INTRODUCTION

"What do you want?" is the second most important question to ask someone. That may leave you asking, "Well then, what is the *most* important question to ask someone?"

My answer is, "What do you *really* want?"

Let me explain why I would make such a bold claim. In my 30 years of leadership experience, I have worked side by side with hundreds of people processing both simple and difficult experiences. The contents of this book began to take shape in July 2010 in a twelve-foot square, wood-paneled office with an old brown chalkboard hanging on one wall. Michael, a handsome, athletic man in his mid-30's, had recently ridden his road bike eight hundred miles across the barren wasteland of Western America from Salt Lake City, Utah to Ashland, Oregon. This Herculean bicycle trek was a last-ditch effort to fix his conflicted life that had been governed by alcohol. His wife had kicked him out of the house. He had lost his job, his driver's license, his children's trust, and almost everything else he ever had enjoyed. Riding his bike across the Western desert he said had felt like riding to the end of the world.

As we worked together through his conflict, we discovered a particular pattern that influenced his behavior. Intrigued by his honesty about his struggles, I documented the details, analyzed the data, and then experimented with the cyclical pattern he repeated. I realized his troubles were not unique and affected more people than those with alcohol problems. Michael revealed an invisible force that directly influenced his daily decisions. As I became more cognizant of this invisible force, I was astonished at the powerful pressure it exerts on all humans, including myself!

The words *I want* express this force profoundly.

Most wants appear to be worthwhile. Some tend to be a bit divisive or short-sighted, while others are visionary and philanthropic. Typically, attached to each want are underlying motives and tactics that people employ to get what they want.

Even more interesting is what happens when people don't get what they want. Over the years, friends, colleagues, and others have freely divulged to me both business and personal conflicts when they weren't getting what they wanted. In positions of trust and responsibility, I had the opportunity to discuss with people just about any question imaginable. I asked a lot of questions, then listened. Eventually, I scrubbed that list of questions down to two.

After listening to a dilemma, I would ask, "*What* do you want?" After several answers, I would refine that list of wants by asking, "What do you *really* want?" Often, those answers were quite different, and then the second question opened the door to deeper introspection with such questions as, "Is what you want now preventing you from obtaining what you really want in the future? Do your wants accept reasonable timing or demand unreasonable urgency? *Why* do you want what you want? Are those desires in harmony with your own values or with those to whom you account—people with whom you connect in your family, organizations, or communities? Are your wants aligned with the goals you share within your most treasured relationships?"

More important than the questions were the answers, which proved to be enlightening. Through the years, I subsequently discussed my list of questions, responses, and observations about wants with business executives and professionals in psychology. I tested the concepts I had discovered both at work and in my own home, then noted the variability of the cause-and-effect relationship between people's wants and their emotions. I learned how emotions can lead to logical or illogical conclusions, how those conclusions may influence reactive or proactive actions, and how all these corresponding principles reveal the power to get more of what people want—or take those wants away. Additional evidence and studies by competent psychologists have substantiated the insights and responses that I have observed firsthand. As I discussed my findings with others and delivered presentations about how wants affect people's lives, an increasing demand has emerged for me to share more of what I was learning with a greater audience.

As someone who cares deeply about people, I hope to offer you insights and patterns about how to increase your awareness of personal wants so you can conscientiously adjust your response to them. As you do, you will discover how to get what you *really* want in life. My goal is to inspire you to observe and organize patterns and then use that newfound awareness to define a better future.

The purpose of this book is first, to help you *recognize* your personal wants with all their intricacies, interdependencies, moral foundations, and worth. This includes not just *what* you want, but *how* and *why* you want those things. Secondly, the methodologies in this book are designed to help you *regulate* your responses to those wants. The application of these principles will promote positive results in all aspects of your life.

*The Invisible Four-letter Word* is organized into three distinct sections.

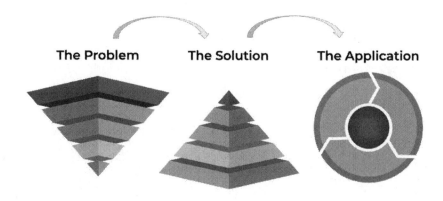

**Section One: The Problem** increases our awareness about how wants motivate us from the moment we are born and the potential complications they can cause. We explore the nature and complexities of wants by introducing The Six Dimensions of Desire and The Choice Spectrum, both of which describe what drives decisions about our wants and how those choices affect others. An upside-down pyramid model shows how conflicting wants can set off a sequence of natural, negative responses that influence our lives and those we love in ways we may not recognize. The problem lies in the disconnect between what we truly desire and our immediate behaviors that lead us elsewhere.

**Section Two: The Solution** uses an upright pyramid model to reveal how regulated responses to our wants can reduce conflict and promote harmony. As we learn to prioritize and sacrifice less-valuable wants, a sequence of favorable responses impacts our lives and the lives of others in rewarding and positive ways.

**Section Three: The Application** outlines the processes for converting upside-down responses into what I call "upright" responses. The action-oriented application section describes the tools we need to produce more sustainable and desirable outcomes, presenting two methodologies to help us create a more stable, connected life that aligns with our highest values. These include:

- **The Core:** a model with four specific conventions that help us regulate our response to our wants

- **The Consensus Diagram:** a tool for identifying the underlying assumptions that provoke conflict and a methodology for rationally resolving differences

Think of this book like a car repair shop. Section one explores why your car is not working well. Section two describes how it should perform when running properly, and section three provides the tools and parts necessary to fix the problems discovered.

Additionally, your car is not the only vehicle in the shop. Because human wants do not exist in a social vacuum, this book explores the connectivity between individuals and their wants. Our motives make the pursuit of happiness and harmony (within ourselves and with others) potentially problematic and complex. When we learn to recognize then regulate our wants, we bring to fruition our deepest desires and empower ourselves to master the future.

# THE PROBLEM

*Wants motivate us from the moment we are born. Conflicting wants can set off a sequence of natural, negative responses that affect our lives and those we love in ways we may fail to recognize. The problem lies in the disconnect between what we truly desire and our immediate behaviors that lead us elsewhere.*

# CHAPTER 1

# THE QUESTION

*"What is necessary to change a person is to change his awareness of himself."*

—Abraham Maslow

Giovanni stopped dead in his tracks as two boys tumbled down the steep stairs and rolled like a ball of yarn across his feet. He stood, appalled at how they fought like wild dogs on the cobblestone. Rousting him out of his deep thoughts, he leapt from the walkway into the street to break up the fight, losing his suede flat cap in the process.

"*Ragazzi!* Boys, stop it!" he yelled, as he grabbed each of them by the back of their coats, tearing them apart. "What is wrong with you?"

The boys, maybe seven or eight, were oblivious to Giovanni's intervention. Their eyes were still locked on each other in combat. Giovanni pinned the boy in his right hand onto the cold cobblestone street. The boy's wild breath blew the dust from between the blocks, breaking his emotional gridlock.

With his left arm, Giovanni pulled the other boy closer and calmly steamed in a low tone, "I said, what is wrong with you?"

"I want the ball, and he won't give it to me," squealed the upright lad.

Lifting the other boy off the cobblestone, Giovanni asked, "Is that true? You won't share your ball with him?"

"It's my ball!" cried the boy with the dirty face.

"Why don't you both play with the ball together?"

"Because it's my ball, and he wants it!" accused the owner, pointing his finger in disgust.

Giovanni released his grip, dropping both boys to the ground simultaneously. Slowly, he stood up, reached for his flat cap, covered his thick black hair, and continued his sad walk down the dingy, narrow street. It took a minute or two before he regained the train of thought that was pulsing through his head before the ridiculous scuffle.

*Ah, yes,* he remembered as he wiped his hands on his wool coat. *What do I do about all the hostility in my community? This fighting is just a symptom of a generation of madness.*

~

Giovanni was mayor of the little village of Pittolo, a quaint community of families living along the Po River in northern Italy. Or rather, it *should* have been quaint, but widespread turmoil among the citizens had turned what used to be a picturesque farming hamlet into a mess of unkempt homes. The people of Pittolo weren't living; they were simply existing. Trash littered the streets. Buildings lay in disrepair. With tensions high, exchanges were strictly business, and even then, their conversations were passionate, Italian-style debates.

It had all begun to unravel thirty years earlier when one of the most influential families in Pittolo wanted to double the size of their pig farm. At the time, they were the largest employer in town. Those who worked at the farm welcomed the growth. However, the other half of the community hated the smell, the dust, and being labeled "the pig town." They opposed the development and wanted it to disappear altogether. The people of Pittolo were not only divided but troubled, with ongoing unrest. As the farmers built pens during the day, others tore them down at night. Conflict

2

escalated, anger increased, and accusations flew from both sides. Eventually, it turned physical: fights erupted, barns were burned, and someone was killed. The village felt unsafe. As crime expanded, goodwill dwindled, and indiscretion filled the gaps. Employment dropped; customers and suppliers stopped coming to town, and the thriving community crumbled to become the senseless mess Giovanni saw before him. The once prosperous pork business and distinguished peace of Pittolo lay in ruin. Everyone felt powerless to do anything but blame each other.

*What can I do?* sighed Giovanni.

~

The next morning, a rapid knock on his wooden door awoke Giovanni. Not sure if it was a dream or not, he lay in his bed, still coming to his senses. The brief knocking came again.

"I'm coming!" growled Giovanni. Donning his robe as he walked, he slipped his arm through a sleeve and opened the door to a dazzling bright day.

"Who is it?" he grumbled, shielding his face. He couldn't even see who was there as the brilliant sun was directly behind the visitor. "Who are you? What do you want?"

A beautiful dark-haired girl with deep brown Italian eyes stepped in, breaking the blindness of the morning. For a moment, a wave of awe overcame Giovanni.

"I am Fausta," the girl proclaimed. "Maestro from Sassolungo sent me to fetch you."

"Maestro? Sassolungo? You mean the mountain? Do I owe him money? What does he want from me?"

Fausta smiled pleasantly as she raised one eyebrow. Drawing closer to his face, she stared deep into his eyes and whispered, "He has a gift—for you!" tapping one finger on his chest.

Stepping back to relieve the discomfort he was feeling, Giovanni pulled his robe around him for security. "A gift? What gift?" His eyes darted about. "What—what are you talking about?"

"It is something you want," she replied. "Something you *really* want." She turned and her dress spun around as she skipped away right into the morning sun.

After a moment, Giovanni snapped out of his daze. Grabbing the frame of the door, he looked after the girl, but she was gone. Leaving the door wide open, Giovanni bolted into his room to dress as quickly as he could. He filled his knapsack with food, extra clothes, and assorted items he would need for a few days' journey. After grabbing his wool coat and hat, he raced through the door, hoping to catch up to the mysterious girl.

Three days later, Giovanni found himself northeast of the Po River, deep in the Dolomite Mountains. His feet hurt, his legs were spent, and his food had run out.

He turned toward Siusi, the last small village before approaching the Sassolungo. As he walked, he noticed the immaculate streets, stunning landscape, brightly colored homes, and charming people who greeted each other warmly, even speaking different languages. He heard German, Italian, and a local dialect he didn't understand. Children played together while the markets bustled with people who looked like they were thriving— even the air seemed filled with harmony. A large group of men gathered for a social game of bocce ball, kissing each other on the cheeks as they met. It was as if Giovanni had been transported into another world.

*"Buongiorno!"* cried a familiar voice from across the street. Fausta enthusiastically waved at Giovanni.

*"Ciao!"* he called, as he quickly tried to cross the street, stepping directly in front of a merchant pushing a handcart. "My apologies!" Giovanni begged as he grabbed the wood frame of the abruptly stopped cart.

"No worries, stranger," came a friendly reply. "Luckily for you it was a leisure walk to the market today. You look lost—and confused. What are you looking for?" the vendor warmly inquired.

"That girl! No, I mean, I am looking for that girl to help me," Giovanni clarified as he looked up from the cart, searching for the beautiful, brown-eyed girl. As quickly as she had appeared, she had vanished again.

"Who are you looking for?" the merchant inquired.

"Fau—I mean Maestro, Maestro of Sassolungo."

"Ah, Maestro!" the man's face lit up, standing a little taller. "Well friend, if you let go of my cart, I can lead you in that direction—if that is where you really want to go."

The two new friends cleared the street and walked to the market at the east end of town, greeting all kinds of friendly people along the way.

"What is this place?" inquired Giovanni.

"It's Siusi!" the merchant proudly exclaimed as he pushed his cart.

"Wait, where were you going before I interrupted your travels?" Giovanni apologized, slightly distracted. "I am so sorry to cause your delay."

"No troubles, my friend. Welcome to Siusi. It is the most peaceful place in the world."

"But you have so many different people here, so many languages, and cultures. And living so near the border ... doesn't any of that cause problems?" Giovanni asked, thinking about his hometown.

"There is very little conflict here. We want more than that. We value harmony. That's why I stopped to help you. As I was making my way to the market, you stepped in front of my path without looking. I wondered if you were lost, or maybe even confused. Only a blind man would step into the street without looking," he teased.

"Yes," agreed Giovanni, "I was slightly distracted.... But why didn't you just yell at me to get out of the way? That seems a little odd. And why are you helping me now? Didn't you say you are on your way to work? Won't you be late?"

The man from Siusi shook his head with a smile, "My friend, so many questions. Let's start with the first. Why wouldn't my first response be to yell? I'll give you the answer: *recognize, then regulate,*" came the explanation.

"What did you say?" Giovanni asked, squinting his eyes.

"That is what Maestros teaches."

"What does it mean? I don't understand."

"It is how we live with kinship in our lovely village. If you want to know more, you will have to ask Maestro," the merchant man urged. "Speaking of Maestro, he lives up there."

Giovanni lifted his eyes and looked to the east where the man pointed toward the white-capped tips of the Sassolungo. "Thank you!" Giovanni beamed with gratitude as he walked toward the peak. Even though his stomach wanted to be fed, what he really wanted was what the mountain had to offer.

Ascending the central path leading up the mountain, Giovanni huffed his way toward the *forcella,* the crotch of the crag. When he reached the gap, he found a flat rock on which to rest from his half-day climb. Exhausted and hungry, he sat down and dropped his head in fatigue.

"Welcome, Giovanni," a warm voice greeted him from behind.

Snapping back into consciousness, he pivoted on the rock to see the brown-eyed girl.

"It's you!" he exclaimed. "How did you get up here before I did?"

"I live here," Fausta graciously replied.

"Oh, you live here? This seems like a rough place to live." Scratching his head, Giovanni looked around at the rugged surroundings. "Ah, I see. You live here with Maestro."

"Thank you for being so determined, so diligent," she smiled.

"Yes, of course," he admitted.

"Your efforts were earnest, but more importantly, you came with a sincere question," Fausta affirmed.

"I did?" A few seconds of silence passed as Giovanni searched his mind for the question that had drawn him to this moment. "I ... I can't remember what it was," he confessed.

"It came the morning when the two boys fought like dogs in the street."

"Two boys?" mumbled Giovanni. *What two boys?* He thought to himself. "Oooh, you mean the two boys who were fighting over a stupid ball? Yes. Yes, I remember it now. My question was, 'What do I do about all the hostility in my community?'"

"Yes, Giovanni, that is the question."

Standing up, Giovanni demanded, "How did you know that was my question? I didn't see you there.... Wait—how do you know what was *only* in my head?"

Stepping closer to him, Fausta began, "There once was a man—a successful man who became a doctor. He lived just north of here, over the border in Germany. Although prosperous, he was dissatisfied with his life. He made a deal with the devil, exchanging his soul for unlimited knowledge and worldly pleasures. In the end, all that knowledge and all the luxuries never granted him satisfaction—those things never offered him what he really wanted."

She turned away from Giovanni to hide her emotions.

"Who was he? Did you know him?" he begged.

After a long moment of silence as she regained her composure, she whispered, "He was my grandfather." Brushing her hair back, she moved closer to Giovanni. "Now, back to your question. What do *you* want?"

With thoughtful intent, Giovanni declared, "I want to know ... what to do ... about all the thoughtless, short-sighted contention in my community." He knelt in front of her. "I just came from Siusi. That is what I am looking for. Siusi. That's what I want for Pittolo. Even more, I want the people of my town to desire the peace and goodwill that I felt in Siusi!"

She reached out and took his hand, "How are you going to do that?"

"That's what I want to know! I can't change people; *they* must want something better, something more than what currently blinds them. How do you get people to see things differently?" Giovanni pleaded.

"Like your people, my grandfather was nearsighted too," Fausta admitted. "You must lift your eyes from the mundane things that lie directly in front of you and look far into the future toward that which is of most worth. It is there, in those sacrificial places, where you envision what you really want. Only then can you begin to recognize and regulate to get there."

A chill ran through Giovanni. "What did you say?"

"Recognize, then regulate, Giovanni," she smiled.

"Recognize and regulate what?" he said more slowly. "What are you talking about?"

"I'm talking about the invisible four-letter word."

# CHAPTER 2

# CONFLICT

*"Everyone thinks of changing the world, but
no one thinks of changing himself."*

—Leo Tolstoy

Who doesn't love people-watching? Studying the interactions between individuals fascinates me. Over the years, I have conducted hundreds of interviews, sat through countless hours of professional meetings, observed stressful situations, and paid particular attention to the leisurely interplay between people. Then I began recording meticulous notes about both positive and negative responses. I earnestly asked about people's initial desires, analyzing and examining their emotional responses, body language, facial expressions, and levels of engagement. Considering the complexities, dependencies, and variabilities of life that affect all of us, I tried to make sense of these observed interactions and learn why people do what they do.

To better understand the basic nature about how people interact with each other, let's examine an analogy of human interplay through the lens of a common intersection design.

Roundabouts direct traffic safely and efficiently at the intersection of two or more roads. Like any intersection, they help drivers proceed to their intended destination after converging at a potential collision point. However, the roundabout's unique design significantly differs from crossroads that are controlled by traffic signals. Stoplights simply instruct motorists when to stop or go. Roundabouts, on the other hand, require each driver to subtly communicate in a split second with the other drivers in order to navigate cooperatively. The continuous flow of traffic becomes seamless and proceeds smoothly when drivers are considerate, collaborative, and aware of each other as they navigate. The essence of the roundabout's simplicity is that it invites each driver to *recognize* then carefully yield to others, facilitating an effective give-and-take response. This prevents the abrupt stops and starts typical of most intersections that otherwise produce inefficient and therefore slower movement toward the drivers' destinations, effectively *regulating* the flow of traffic peacefully and avoiding conflicts.

Our approach, attitude, and reactions to others already in the roundabout (and those who are entering it) can make a dramatic difference in outcomes. Conflict may develop when a single driver stops paying attention to their surroundings, acts thoughtlessly, proceeds impulsively, or applies bad judgment. One reckless person could disrupt the synergistic flow of this streamlined intersection. It's not the transportation engineer's fault that an accident happens in a roundabout. When individuals fail to live up to the principles inherent to the road's design, they constrain or defy the roundabout's intended performance and purpose, which inevitably leads to conflict.

A roundabout is analogous to the interactions we encounter as we journey through life. We each come from distinct places and have various destinations. Throughout our individual journeys, we not only touch each other's lives, but we engage and affect each other in positive and negative ways. Our capacity to navigate those intersections—including the ability to consider, calculate, and work toward our own path's destination—uniquely defines us as humans. As we steer our way through life's roundabouts, are we using a harmonious approach to promote positive progress, working to keep the entire system flowing properly? Do we choose to work cooperatively with others as our paths cross? Are we using situational awareness and understanding as we collaborate with others? Conversely, are there times when we cause conflict as we bulldoze our way into the social roundabouts of life?

Working together requires each of us to observe, yield, merge, go with the flow, and then signal our intentions to others as we continue. The choices we make in these pivotal moments of life play a significant role in whether or not we get what we want and how much conflict occurs along the way.

What do you want? What do you *really* want?

# The Invisible Four-letter Word

Beyond simply arriving at our destination, we want to prosper and be happy. But the pursuit of success and lasting joy has a high correlation with putting off something now for something better in the future. That "something" is the focus of this book—it is what I call *the invisible four-letter word*. The invisible four-letter word is WANT. It is invisible because we don't always recognize how our wants drive our behaviors, and because often we are blind to how our responses to those wants affect others.

To want is to feel a need or a desire for something. Wants are the things you wish for, long for, crave, demand, or desire. Behind all your behaviors are the wants that drive them—typically undetected beneath the surface.

"Want" can be used as either a verb or a noun: the act of wanting (verb) or the things (noun) we want. Both meanings apply in our discussion of this invisible force that affects almost every aspect of our lives.

In my years of studying the concept of *want* and my tenacious quest to make sense of it, I concluded that *what* we want and also *how* we want play a significant role in both our intended and unintended future. This "want hypothesis" burst into focus after my friend Michael and I began working on his problem together. As we sifted through his challenging situation, his deeply descriptive feelings and subsequent responses expanded my consideration. Michael changed my life. The profound experience that unfolded with Michael formulated the foundational concepts in this book.

The discovery of the invisible four-letter word inspired the process of response regulation, which explains how *harmony within us and with others (and therefore the degree to which we flourish) increases as we learn to* **recognize** *then* **regulate** *the natural struggle that exists between conflicting wants in their various forms, the diverse wants of others, and our responses to those wants.*

But before we explore the nature of *want* and our responses to those desires, let me tell Michael's story about how we discovered the invisible four-letter word.

## Michael's Painful Exclamation

When I initially met Michael after he biked to Oregon, he was homeless, hungover, and barely conscious of the tent he was sleeping in, let alone his existence. Seeking help, his sister called me the morning after his arrival to her home, concerned about his destitute and drunken situation. Her desperate tone prompted me to go to her house immediately, where I found Michael lying on a cot in a tent in her backyard. That first interaction with Michael was brief as he struggled to sit up and have a coherent conversation.

The stars aligned, and we quickly became friends. For the next one-and-a-half years, I spent countless hours attempting to help Michael overcome his dependency on alcohol. "Attempting" is the most appropriate word because I didn't do a very good job of helping him alter his life. As much as I wanted to help his situation, and no matter how much he wanted to change, he didn't know *how* to change.

---

Both *what* we want and *how* we want play a
significant role in both our intended and
unintended future.

---

During that same time, I happened to be reading a *New York Times* bestseller book, *Influencer*, so I studied that book to see how its principles might help me affect a change in Michael's life.[1] I put more work into trying to help Michael than I had with anyone else. Yet, no matter how hard I tried to influence him, Michael turned back to alcohol every few weeks. Repeatedly, he lost his employment and was evicted from his apartment. *How many times can a person hit rock bottom?* I asked myself. Despite my efforts, I couldn't influence him to change.

After more than a year of working with Michael, I took him to Delancey Street in San Francisco. Delancey Street is a residential self-help organization established in 1971 and was featured in the book *Influencer*. They teach substance abusers who have run out of options how to turn their lives around. I reasoned that if I couldn't help Michael change, perhaps they could.

Before I took Michael to Delancey Street, I pulled him into my office to have a serious chat. It was a Saturday morning after a difficult week of dealing with his addiction. One night after moving in with my family, he took my truck to purchase some cheap vodka, then he drank the whole bottle and passed out in the front seat. I spent hours that night driving around town looking for Michael and my truck, hoping they both were intact. You can imagine my indignation when I found him. It was time for a deliberate conversation about his decisions, and I was ready to do whatever it took to find the source of this unacceptable behavior.

"Michael," I began, "you know that I love you, and that I want to help you in every way imaginable."

"Yes," he said with quiet humility, staring at the blue-carpeted floor.

"Why? Why do you do this? What is the root cause of all your drinking?" I pleaded earnestly.

After a long moment of silent contemplation, he groaned, "I feel like I'm buried under the tip of an upside-down pyramid. Its massive weight is crushing my chest. I can't breathe."

Without sympathy I rebutted, "Wait, Michael, come on. Pyramids can't be upside down. They would fall over. An upside-down pyramid is not sustainable."

Looking up from the carpet, he gazed deep into my eyes for several silent seconds. Then, leaning forward, he painfully exclaimed, "That's my point!"

My soul melted with compassion. I proceeded with more mercy as I listened and learned. What followed was a spark of inspiration toward real, personal change. We explored why Michael's life was, as he said, "upside down." I asked a lot of questions, seeking to understand the reason this pressure-producing pyramid existed. A beautiful diagram unfolded from our discussion and found its way onto the chalkboard.

What we discovered together over the next several, soul-searching hours was the root of his problem. As we combed through the granularity of his troubles, one immense impediment emerged. When I repeatedly asked him why he felt upside down, we discovered *the invisible four-letter word*—WANT. After identifying that word and why it caused him to feel upside down, we both had an aha moment.

## Turning Pain into Purpose

Following that rich revelation with Michael, I initiated discussions with other people who expressed feeling "upside down" because of personal conflict or other struggles. I inquired about the relationship between feeling unsettled and the wants that perpetuated those feelings. The more I explored, the more I noticed the same pattern for most of the problems and disputes being revealed. The things I discovered over months of analysis and testing helped unravel general disagreements. I found that I could help relieve struggles between individuals and reduce conflicts between people and entities, such as issues arising between employees and company policies or processes.

My personal life changed as well. Once I understood the power of the invisible four-letter word, my ability to reduce contention and change outcomes in my own life drastically improved.

When you understand and recognize the correlation between your wants and the positive or negative reactions to those desires, you too will notice predictable patterns. Great power comes from knowing that your wants become a fuse that sets off a sequence of other behavioral fireworks—both good and bad. Wants can drive and inspire us to do fantastic things, or they can insidiously lead us into conflict.

# The Conflict of Opposing Wants

The conflict of opposing wants has existed from the beginning of time. For example, if one partner wants a dog, but the other partner does not, they have a conflict. One owner of the business wants to source products from overseas while the other wants to manufacture them domestically. While some disputes are over simple preferences, others don't make as much sense. In fact, studies indicate that some people intentionally try to incite conflict just to gain attention.[2]

But, despite all the contention in the world, opposition does not have to be viewed as a bad thing. William Ellery Channing, a prominent Unitarian preacher of the nineteenth century, noted, "Difficulties are meant to rouse, not discourage. The human spirit is to grow strong by conflict."[3]

If conflict is supposed to make us stronger, how can we turn it into something meaningful? Phil Knight of Nike insightfully stated, "There is an immutable conflict at work, in life, and in business—a constant battle between peace and chaos. Neither can be mastered, but both can be influenced. How you go about that is the key to success."[4]

Let's take Phil Knight's success challenge, increase our power to reduce conflict, and start making peace out of chaos. As we unveil the invisible nature of our desires, we begin the process of becoming aware of our wants and recognizing how adjustments and responses to those wants can help us solve conflict rather than create it.

# CHAPTER 3

# THE NATURE OF "WANT"

*"What we want in life is the greatest
indication of who we really are."*

—Richard Paul Evans

*Want* is the invisible force that propels us through the persistent press of time, dragging us from one moment to the next. This push and pull action shifts us from one want to another. Because wants are as plentiful as people on the planet, the act of wanting sees no end. What complicates the nature of wants is the interconnectedness of people in the world with their various desires, which are invisible to most people. How do we harness the power of this invisible drive into something we can use to our benefit? The first step is to turn on our awareness.

Do we really know what we want?

We must put on new glasses. Wake up. Pay closer attention to what we want and how we respond to various wants. For example, perhaps you want to sleep in, but you also want to be responsible. Your son has a basketball game tonight, but you would rather go to happy hour. You enjoy checking social media, but you also want to be productive. You keep maxing out your credit card but also want to retire early. You avoid taking initiative yet hope for a promotion.

These examples reveal that sometimes we inadvertently allow our superficial wants to displace our true desires.[1] We've all heard someone ask, "How did I end up here?" This question indicates the invisible nature of wants. Let's look at some other forms of wants.

# The Many Faces of Want

Wants appear in a variety of packages that may masquerade as other things. For example, the blatant "I want" statement is as easy to spot as a bride in a biker's bar. "I don't want" statements are a little trickier. If I don't want one thing, I likely *do* want something else. For example, "I don't want to go out tonight" probably translates into "I want to stay home." There is the famous interaction when, after hours in the car, someone in the car asks, "Do you want to stop for a break?" My answer is "no." But they aren't really asking about what *I* want. Rather, they are trying to communicate that *they* want to stop for a bathroom break. That's what the person really means.

Some desires also can be expressed in silent forms such as longing or resistance. For example, we might simply ignore what's said and quietly do whatever *we* want to do. This silent defiance can poison personal, social, and work relationships, leading to ineffectiveness. Sometimes we remain quiet because we have private or personal wants that are positive, but they are not in line with those around us or appropriate to share. Our silence protects our personal goals from the negative scrutiny or judgment of others.

More subtle ways of expressing the act of wanting are listed below. These include both spoken and non-verbal cues and behaviors that can be expressed, felt, or acted out. Here are a few examples of each:

| | |
|---|---|
| I need … | I don't care. |
| My desire is … | I've had a manifestation. |
| My expectations are … | I hate … |
| I would rather (or rather not) … | I despise … |
| I feel … | I'm inclined to … |
| I choose to … | Can you get that for me? |
| I have to … | That's not me. |
| I'm not going to … | I wish … |
| I don't do … | I dislike … |
| I'm craving … | There's no way I would … |
| I'm not that kind of a person. | I can't … |
| No! | Yes, but … |
| That's insufficient. | Non-verbal resistance |
| I love … | Withdrawal |
| I prefer not to … | Pointing |
| I prefer to … | Indifference |

This diverse list of expressions and behaviors demonstrates the creative ways in which we convey our wants and try to disguise them from other people. We sometimes mask our wants by behaving courteously or hinting at our wants without declaring them outright; we may or may not even realize we are doing it.

## Wants and Needs

Abraham Maslow conducted research that concluded with *The Theory of Human Motivation.*[2] He believed an individual's *conquering* of their own wants related directly to their satisfaction in life and ability to become their best self. The key is in the conquering—which means that we learn to self-regulate those wants to become our best selves.

Let's briefly review his theory. Needs are the basic requirements necessary for survival, growth, and development. Maslow categorized these needs into five ordered components: physiological, safety, love/belonging, esteem, and self-actualization. Physiological needs include things like food, water, air, and shelter. Safety means security, stability, and protection. Love/belonging consists of social interaction, relationships, and a sense of community. Esteem includes the need for recognition, achievement, and self-respect. Self-actualization refers to the need for personal growth and development.

---

*Want* is the invisible force that propels us through the persistent press of time.

---

While wants may germinate from needs, they often grow beyond needs and are not essential for survival. Culture, societal norms, and personal preferences influence our list of wants that may include material possessions like a new car or a bigger house, or they can include intangible things such as recognition, power, or status.

While Maslow asserted that needs are essential for survival and growth, wants are optional and variable based on personalities, ambitions, and our environment, etcetera. Maslow discovered that the discrepancy between wants and needs can be explained through the nature and the development of our brains. Human brains from infancy to age two are very similar to animal brains because they are almost solely concerned with satisfying immediate needs and are incapable of thinking about future wants.[3] As we develop, we gain the ability to choose and prioritize our needs and delineate our wants.

As humans mature, our capacity to manage, regulate, and delay pressing wants increases. If we fail to learn that regulation, our basic needs can become insatiable, consequently distorting our perception of what we *actually* need, while wants take on a life of their own. In other words, what starts as a basic need can grow out of control and become a want pretending to be a need. That is where the conquering that Maslow mentions must be managed to cultivate our best selves.

Understanding the complexities of our wants (and our tendency to twist them to fit our yearnings) helps us recognize how *wants* drive even the smallest decisions in our lives. With that insight, we learn to respond to our wants more intentionally, and only then can our wants lead us to our ultimate desires. When multiple choices emerge, decisions must be made and some wants sacrificed for others. This is where we must consider the multi-dimensional nature of our wants and how they play into the evaluation and prioritization of our options.

# Six Dimensions of Desire

What lies beneath *want?* To have any chance of increasing awareness of our wants and untangling the complex web of their interconnectedness with other people, we must consider the various dimensions that affect and define our desires. While more dimensions of desire may exist, we explore the following six:

- **Ego:** The degree to which our wants are centered on ourselves or on others (Does this want take into consideration the needs of others [those affected by my response to this want] or only my own?)

- **Intensity:** The energy we feel toward our wants, whether we are extremely passionate about pursuing them or altogether apathetic (What level of resources and dedication am I willing to expend, or to what lengths will I go, to get what I want?)

- **Interval:** The timeframe in which our wants reside (Am I filled with urgency, or can I be patient with the outcome? Is the want fleeting or long lasting?)

- **Worth:** The value we assign to our wants based on our preference, situation, and willingness to sacrifice for it (What value do I put on this desire compared to the alternatives?)

- **Discipline**: The exercise of self-control over our wants that we employ to improve our physical, mental, social, intellectual, or financial well-being (Does this want help me move toward order and improvement, or does my want lead to more chaos?)

- **Ethics:** The moral values, beliefs, or standards that drive our wants (To whom do I answer for my wants, or what values do I use to judge my wants? Do I answer only to myself, or do I hold myself accountable to another identity, a group, a nation, a set of beliefs, or a higher authority such as God?)

Think of these dimensions as separate sliders on a control board of desire. They work together and remain interrelated. Some of these conditions are subordinate to others depending on the results we may seek in any given circumstance. Understanding these Six Dimensions of Desire helps increase our awareness, evaluate our wants, and envision the results of our choices.

Imagine a control board with volume, balance, treble, and bass knobs. While it is undeniably true that we can adjust each slider any way we want, there comes a point where the sound coming out of the system will be unpleasant. Likewise, we can adjust the sliders differently to develop a more pleasing tone.

There is no "right" setting that always works, which means that every situation requires judicious adjustment of each slider. The sliders must remain variable to be tuned according to what is best for the circumstances, weighing the goals we share with others, our potential safety, and the standards we value. For example, some goals may require our passion to be "all in" to achieve them—such as earning a doctorate degree. Conversely, when someone makes an offensive comment, responding empathetically or without reaction to that offense may help us progress beyond the sting rather than choosing to retaliate.

Evaluating and prioritizing wants produce common-sense balance. For example, adjusting the ego slider all the way to "selfish," like adopting an "I can do whatever I want" philosophy, may get us what we want temporarily, but eventually, that extreme setting will cause conflict. Yet, sliding the ego all the way to "selfless" all the time can also be dangerous.

The control board example simply illustrates the contingent, layered, and complex nature of our wants, and this discussion only briefly addresses these dimensions. Taking time to ponder the Six Dimensions of Desire and how they affect personal effectiveness offers valuable insight about our behaviors. Referring back to the Richard Paul Evans quotation at the beginning of this chapter, I would add that it's not only *what* we want in life—but *how* and *why* we want it—that becomes the greatest indication of who we really are.

Obviously, this book cannot address every want a person may have, especially extreme scenarios. Analyzing the slider position on your own control board of desire can help you recognize the true position and influence of your wants.

## Where Wants Lead

Think back to Giovanni's story from chapter 1. Dissecting the characters' wants helps us analyze and evaluate both the invisible and visible nature of wants. From that analysis we can project where those desires may lead. In the story, two communities stand in contrast: problematic Pittolo and serene Siusi. Pittolo was racked with contention and division. The people of Pittolo set their sliders one way, while the people of Siusi adjusted them in other ways, and thus we see the relationship between certain settings that subsequently cause harmony or discord.

Below is a list of questions you can use to explore the Six Dimensions of Desire more thoroughly within the story. Examining the questions below may be mostly rhetorical. Their purpose is to help you visualize the causes and effects of wants and how they influence conflict.

- The story describes how some of the citizens of Pittolo wanted to expand their pig farm while others did not want the farm to change. Did the farmers consider how the expansion may impact the villagers who opposed it? Did the people resisting the change consider the economic potential of the expansion?

- How did the Pittolo citizens' consideration or lack thereof indicate the level of ego in their responses or the relative worth they placed on the farm? How might an adjustment to those considerations have changed the situation?

- How did the conflict in Pittolo affect the emotions of the people on both sides of the argument? In their heightened emotional state, were all citizens demonstrating mutual respect in their responses and actions as the disagreements ensued?

- Why does holding onto negative emotion lead to decay of consideration over time?

- What responses might have changed the direction of the interactions in Pittolo? What relatively small, incremental choices could have either magnified or de-escalated the issue?

- What was the long-term result of the Pittolo citizens' ongoing dispute and lack of consideration for each other?

- How could their early responses have contributed to the consequential powerlessness and uninviting culture that prevailed in Pittolo at the time of the story?

- How might the results have differed if the people had tried earnestly to find common ground in their shared desire for a good life in Pittolo—rather than focusing on their divided opinions?

- What attributes and behaviors may have blinded the people of Pittolo and left them wallowing in the bondage of conflict?

- Not far away, Siusi was a vibrant, bustling, economic pulse of activity filled with liveliness. Siusi enjoyed cultural diversity and yet harmonized their differences. How might the citizens' general regard for others, sacrifice, and goodwill have come about? How could their personal choices and concern about conflict have possibly contributed to the town's charm, welcoming nature, and culture of peace?

- What common thread interconnected the people of Siusi? Could it be that their desire to maintain their long-term, shared values of respect and peace overcame their (less important) differences?

These two villages radically differed—but what differentiated them? What traits and habits did Siusi residents employ that may have inspired them to work for and maintain a positive and uplifting culture? Conversely, what prevailing attitudes may have gripped Pittolo that kept them stuck in an ongoing cycle of strife? Could Pittolo have had a more positive outcome in their town had they been willing to balance their control sliders differently?

Where we go in life ultimately depends on how we take control of our dimensions of desire as we make choices for ourselves and interact with others.

## Choice, Free Will, and Wants

What drives our desires and makes them good or bad, helpful or detrimental, regulated or unregulated? Fundamental to our desires, our inherent free will as humans bestows on us the responsibility of choice.

Free will is the uniquely human ability to make complex, cognitive decisions.[4] Saul Mcleod, PhD describes free will when he declares that "...we are free from the causal influences of past events. According to free will a person is responsible for their own actions."[5]

No other creature on planet Earth possesses the decisive processing power that belongs to humankind.[6] The exclusive endowments of reason, sympathy, passion, and morality separate us from every other living organism.[7] No other animal can improve its current condition like humans. Deepak Chopra wisely points out that "When you make a choice, you change the future." Cars, electricity, homes, tools, and technology all exist because of humankind's superior capacity to both reason and choose. We have yet to discover a polar bear who decides to take a well-deserved vacation from the bitter Arctic Sea to visit the Bahamas. Animals do indeed choose, but not with the same capacity, logic, or complexity as humans.

How does this relate to your choices? The purpose of exploring the concept of choice is to inspire you to take your unique gift of free will and use it to apply the principles taught throughout this book. Your choices surrounding your wants can lead to greater harmony, influence, respect, and honor, all of which contribute to less conflict and more happiness. Your positive choices also build emotional independence, so you become less affected by drama, hatred, strife, animosity, and turmoil. To better understand these connections, let's examine *The Choice Spectrum*.

## The Choice Spectrum

Our wants have little personalities, and they live on a continuum where they jockey for position. The more demanding, impetuous wants try to shove the docile and benevolent wants out of line. The Choice Spectrum helps pinpoint where those wants stand on the spectrum and which way they may be facing. Identifying their position and ambition helps us make good, better, or best choices with the many wants that run in and out of our lives.

The Choice Spectrum displays a horizontal line with arrows pointing in opposite directions. *Self* is at the center where our most basic wants and needs exist. Those opposite facing arrows overlap in the center, representing a balanced blend of both selfless *and* selfish wants. For example, at a family gathering, I am hungry and want food, but I have enough control to allow my grandmother to be served first.

Before exploring each side of The Choice Spectrum, let me establish my intent. Like any spectrum, there is a left and right side. The Choice Spectrum is not a political statement, nor is it a play on party lines.

These wants in the center go with the flow, don't cause excessive problems, and are generally considerate. Stories about these wants don't show up in the newspaper or on the evening news. These wants don't go out of their way to help their neighbors, nor do they call the cops on them. They go to work, collect a paycheck, pay their mortgage on time, watch some TV, go to bed, and do it all over again the next day. Typically, this casual blend of selfish and selfless wants at the center of the Choice Spectrum are not necessarily wrong.

Using probability theory, we can surmise that roughly 68 percent of our wants lie somewhere in the middle of the Choice Spectrum.[8] The normal distribution bell curve provides a visual representation along the continuum. This is not an actual sampling of scientific data but is an idealized probability to help illustrate the principle.

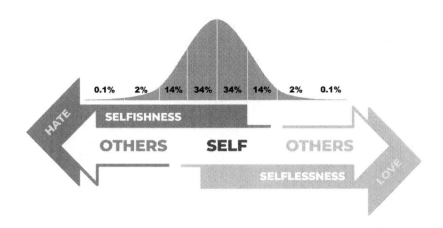

The wants at the center of the choice spectrum are the familiar, commonplace wants we entertain every day. However, when our wants stray from the middle in either direction, life becomes more interesting. The more distance a want travels to one end or the other, the more notoriety they accumulate for good or ill—similar to the extreme adjustments we can make with the Six Dimensions of Desire.

---

Where we go in life ultimately depends
on how we take control of our
dimensions of desire.

---

### What do the two sides of The Choice Spectrum represent?

Increasing degrees of self-*ish*-ness and hatred define the wants on the left side of the Choice Spectrum. The further a want travels in this direction, the less consideration it has for others and the more it delights in disrupting other wants. Intensely selfish wants do as they please, ignoring how their actions affect others. The most selfish wants promote themselves and perpetuate a scarcity mindset while taking freedom away from others. They seek to tear things down and dismantle competing ideas. Over-crowded prisons and fallen civilizations provide evidence of this pattern.

Stephen Kendrick suggests, "Almost every sinful action ever committed can be traced back to a selfish motive. It is a trait we hate in other people but justify in ourselves."[9]

Selfish wants on the far end of this spectrum become famous for their fiendish influence. At the extremity, we find the notorious .01 percent such as Pol Pot, Ivan the terrible, Joseph Stalin, and Adolf Hitler, who all showed how the satisfaction of their personal wants came at the price of other's lives.

Conversely, on the right side of the spectrum, we find degrees of self-*less*-ness. As these wants progress to the right, generosity and love toward others intensify. These wants are open to alternative perspectives and consider what others want. Selfless wants embrace the abundance mentality and willingly migrate to this end of the spectrum. Generous wants uplift and encourage others, ratifying their love and genuine concern. Charles Dickens said, "No one is useless in this world who lightens the burden of another."

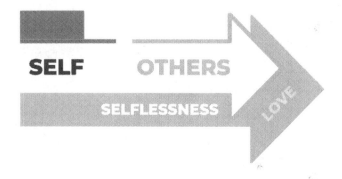

The further a want moves to the right, the more it goes out of its way to provide relief and lend assistance. These wants stop for strangers to change a flat tire. They strive for peace, friendship, and tranquility. They build bridges across the chasm of hatred and courageously fight for freedom. The further a want moves toward selflessness, the more charity it has for others, exercising philanthropic enthusiasm to sacrifice and assist. At the extreme .01 percent end, we find some of the most prominent, upright, and loving figures in recorded history such as Martin Luther King, Corrie ten Boom, Gandhi, and Jesus.

Jesus taught his followers to pray to God saying, "Thy *will* be done."[10] Will equals want. Jesus wanted what his Father wanted. The satisfaction of God's want came at the price of Jesus' own life when he declared,

"Greater *love* hath no man than this, that a man lay down his life for his friends."[11] Like Martin Luther King, Corrie ten Boom, Gandhi, and Jesus, love and selflessness govern the wants of altruistic people, leading them to positions of influence and respect.

**What does The Choice Spectrum reveal?** Love and hate regulate the focus of our wants, our emotions, and what we choose to do with them. The Choice Spectrum begins with you in the center. As you embrace wants in either direction, those choices affect other people (even if you don't *want* them to). On one end of the spectrum are people such as scam artists who prey on the retirement savings of innocent elderly people. On the other end of the spectrum, we find examples like doctors and dentists who travel to third-world countries at their own expense, helping those in need of medical and dental care.

Consider where you are on The Choice Spectrum. Which way are you facing? Where would you like to be on the spectrum? What degree of love/selflessness or hate/selfishness expresses your interactions with other people? Do your wants create conflict, or do they promote peace?

You have the power to choose!

# The Power and Potential of Wants

Recalling the roundabout analogy, how would you describe the way you navigate the intersections of your life? Are you living a life that flows smoothly and harmoniously as you interact with other people? What could you achieve if you minimized delays, difficulties, and conflict when you come to crossroads? Imagine the possibility of getting to where you really want to go in life—not a superficial place or one that is part way between here and there. I am talking about way out there—the real destination.

In the theme song from *Mahogany*, "Do You Know Where You're Going To," Diana Ross asks these piercing questions:

Do you know where you're going to?
Do you like the things that life is showing you?
Where are you going to?
Do you know?
Do you get what you're hoping for?
When you look behind you, there's no open doors.
What are you hoping for?
Do you know? [12]

Do you know what is holding you back from achieving the highest potential in your job, in your personal relationships, and in making meaningful contributions in your community? Even more, have you identified the barriers that prevent you from obtaining what you really want?

Giovanni knew full well what he *didn't* want. He disliked the discord of his hometown of Pittolo, and he caught a glimpse of what he really wanted as he walked the friendly streets of Siusi. Giovanni envisioned where he wanted to go but did not know how to get there. It was Fausta who inspired him to "… look far into the future, toward that which is of most worth. It is there, in those sacrificial places, where you envision what you really want. Only then can you begin to recognize and regulate to get there."

When you stop to consider your various wants and recognize them for what they really are, you stand a better chance of regulating them and using them to your benefit. You might ask yourself the second-most important question: *what do I want?* After making your list of answers, drill down and get more specific. Ask yourself the world's most important question, "What do I *really* want?"

An introspective answer to this poignant question could empower your life—if you *want* it to. Keep in mind this truth from Leo Tolstoy: "Everyone thinks of changing the world, but no one thinks of changing himself." A powerful evolution begins when you decide to change yourself rather than trying to change those around you. As you learn to recognize and regulate the many dimensions of your wants every day, then true growth occurs incrementally over time—cultivating your character in positive ways.

Channeling the power of choice propels us toward our most strategic desires. On a personal level, your progress could lead to better physical and mental health as you find more purpose in your goals. Your career could become more fulfilling because you focus on what really matters. Your relationships with friends and family could become stronger as you interact with them in more positive ways. A greater degree of resilience and poise could be yours as you face life's challenges with more fortitude and confidence. Your gratitude for others might increase along with your overall sense of joy. A renewed mindset may propel you toward your vision of who you want to be.

On an organizational level, you may become more of a team player as you pause more often and listen to others with patience and consideration. You could add to the positive nature of your business as your cooperation with and support for others expands with your newfound openness. In this positive environment, contributions, ideas, opinions, and innovations could flourish like never before. Aligning desires and shared goals in organizations produces a cohesion that enables people and systems to reach their full potential—as they shed the pettiness of divisive wants and embrace trust and harmony. The proactive blending of diverse desires creates more harmonious communities at every level, making the world around you a better place. This kind of mindset is contagious, inspiring others to want to follow your lead.

Change yourself and you will change the world.

# CHAPTER 4

# THE UPSIDE-DOWN PYRAMID

*"I guess I've always lived upside down
when I want things I can't have."*

—Tom Waits

"I feel upside down" is a common idiom in the English language. Why would we say such a thing? Turning something over so the top becomes the bottom often throws it into disorder or confusion. Inverting a physical pyramid requires extra effort to keep it propped up. Even if that concept was carefully planned out and executed, upside-down pyramids remain vastly more unstable than upright pyramids! In a world where sustainability has high value, no one invests in a pyramid proposed to be upside down. Not only would it lack longevity, but it also would be unreliable, unmaintainable, uncertain, and unstable.

All of us *feel* upside down from time to time. The emotions we often experience when our wants conflict with others, or when they create dissonance, lead to feeling inverted for a minute or two or for extended periods of time.

## Your Personal Conflict Experience

Throughout the rest of this book, a personal conflict identified from your own life will help you understand, explore, and consider the principles of wants as they are explained. Take a moment to describe a difficulty or disagreement from your personal life that is challenging you right now. It could be contention between you and a family member or a struggle with your partner. Perhaps you deal with a rival at work. Is there someone or something you wrestle to understand? Is conflict stewing inside you? Are you challenged with a controversial decision, battling a bad habit, or facing a moral dilemma?

Once you have a specific conflict experience in mind, take some time to write about it. Record specific details about what you want and how it clashes with another goal you have or what someone else wants. To help you accomplish this, answer each of the following questions with a full sentence or more. You will refer to this experience throughout the book in gray boxes entitled "Connecting the Principles."

What do I want that lies at the heart of my conflict, and why do I want it? ("I want ... because ...")

_____

_____

_____

How do I feel about not getting what I want? ("I feel ... because ...")

_____

_____

_____

What conclusions am I drawing from the emotions I feel about this conflict? (I think ... because...)

_____

_____

_____

How am I reacting to this conflict? (I am doing ... because...)

_____

_____

_____

Am I getting what I want from this conflict? In the end, what do I _really_ want to happen?

_____

_____

_____

# The Upside-down Perspective

Imagine being dropped onto the flat surface of an inverted pyramid. Of necessity, you must position yourself in the center with both hands out like a tightrope walker as you attempt to balance the unstable structure beneath you.

Wobbling around in the center of this metaphorical pyramid, what can you see below you? You can't see *anything* directly underneath you except the sprawling, inverted base of the pyramid on which you stand. The flat surface obstructs your vision, making it impossible to see beyond the edges. If you move to the edge to see beyond it, the whole thing will get out of balance and begin to topple. To keep it in balance, you must stay in the center. With a limited perspective, could you be blind to what is going on around you and be tempted to make assumptions about what is happening beneath you?

Similarly, have you ever encountered someone who seems to disregard other viewpoints or are blind to what they can't see? Or people who only want what *they* want without consideration?

While it is easy to be critical of others who seem upside down and to scrutinize their short-sightedness, we all get caught up in various forms of false premises. For example, belief bias becomes one of those blinders that we all experience to some degree. Belief bias annuls truths we don't like while twisting into facts the assumptions we *do* like. Despite our passion, belief in something doesn't automatically make it true.[1] This type of self-deception can inhibit our view atop the upside-down pyramid or set us on top of it if we weren't already there. Another pitfall is arrogant ignorance, which is where our pride prevents us from considering new information or perspectives because we arrogantly ignore what we don't know.

To be clear, this upside-down perspective typically describes a temporary state of being we all experience when our wants run wild. For some, an upside-down habit can turn into a lifestyle.

Limited perspectives are just the tip of the iceberg. Our unregulated wants impact our perspective and set in motion a chain reaction, which we illustrate through the upside-down pyramid metaphor.

# The Upside-down Pyramid Sequence

The upside-down pyramid contains five fundamental segments describing a sequence of natural human tendencies. Together, the five segments create a pattern of *responses to unregulated wants* that we may not fully recognize. These include:

1. Unregulated Wants

2. Negative Emotions

3. Irrational Conclusions

4. Reactive Responses

5. Powerless Position

As we explore this upside-down, cause-and-effect metaphor, keep in mind the personal conflict experience you wrote about earlier and the Six Dimensions of Desire. How do your wants affect you in both positive and negative ways?

## Segment 1. Unregulated Wants

*Unregulated Wants* dominate the top of the upside-down pyramid model. Of the five segments, *unregulated wants* take up the most real estate. The wants at the top of this pyramid usually consist of the unconstrained wants right in front of us that beg for attention and promote themselves as justifiably important. Depending on the situation, they often (though not always) include the short-term, selfish, urgent, worthless, chaotic, or unethical wants dancing before us. While intentional human desires drive the direction of our lives, uncontrolled, invisible wants can take us places we never intended to go. Uncontrolled wants can create a disproportionate imbalance in our lives.

Every one of us has wants—things we yearn for, that motivate us, or that bring us pleasure or rewards. Some wants, like food and fuel, recur and need to be continually refilled. Other wants don't need to be satiated as often (like frivolous shopping, scrolling through social media, gaming, or watching movies). Marketing geniuses know how to play on our natural desires, and they promote their products by asking the second-most powerful question, "What do you want?"

**Unregulated Wants**

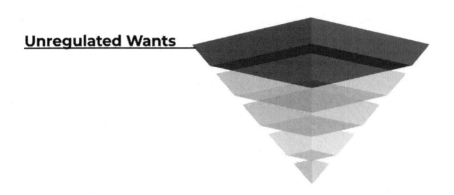

Wants, desires, cravings, expectations, requirements, demands, liking, and longing: all these words mean essentially the same thing—those feelings, that can be either visible or invisible, pulsing within us that move us to act for better or for worse. Recognition and choice make all the difference.

Don't misunderstand—I am not declaring that all wants are bad. Our lives are not upside down simply because we want; rather, it is the *unrecognized* and *unregulated* pursuit of our wants that leads us to trouble. Further, being upside down is *not* an identity, a permanent label, a condemnation, a perpetual state of being, or a final sentencing, and it does not define who we are. As stated earlier, we are driven by wants, moment by moment. *It is the unbridled and often invisible wants that consciously or unconsciously create the broad segment at the top of the upside-down pyramid.*

Additionally, there is a difference between what we want and what we like.[2] For example, we may not want to smoke, but we like to smoke. We may not want a speeding ticket, but we like how it feels to drive fast. We want to get an A on the exam, but we like the distractions on our phones. If what we like takes control over what we want, then those likes become upside-down wants at the top of the inverted pyramid.

The conflict and contention potentially caused by wanting is so widespread between humans that it makes the top ten list of Judeo-Christian commandments: "Thou shalt not covet" is the tenth.[3] The Hebrew word for *covet* (חָמַד châmad) means to desire, lust, or to want something that isn't rightfully yours.[4] The biblical commentary following the tenth commandment gets more specific. Let's substitute *covet* with *want*: "Thou shalt not *want* thy neighbor's house (substances and goods), thou shalt not *want* thy neighbor's wife (sexual relationships), nor his manservant, nor his maidservant (personal resources), nor his ox (tools and equipment), nor his ass (vehicle or other forms of transportation), nor anything that is thy neighbor's."[5] That pretty much covers anything we could ever want! God knows that the misuse of our wants won't culminate in what we truly desire—and that unregulated, wrongful, inappropriate, or selfish wants only bring temporary happiness and can lead to conflict with others. Yet, in the New Testament, Paul counsels us to "Covet earnestly the best gifts."[6] So what are we to believe with this seeming contradiction—we should not covet, or we should *covet earnestly* (zealously pursue) the best gifts?

---

What we *think* we want right now can prevent us from achieving what we really want in the future.

---

It's not necessarily the coveting (wanting) itself that is the problem, but rather what we want and the regulation, ego, ethics, and/or timing of those wants that need to be disciplined.

The wants at the top of the upside-down pyramid are meant to represent the unrestrained, more emotional wants that blind us from remembering what we *really* want.[7] Impetuous wants often constrain our more sensible desires. For example, a teenager erupts when his dad tells him to mow the lawn. He doesn't want to mow the lawn. He wants to be with his friends. But, deep inside, what he *really* wants is to maintain his father's trust. So how can he remember that desire when his friends are waiting with their bikes on the lawn that he is supposed to mow?

A coworker passively rebels by slacking off at work after she doesn't get the raise she wants. But wasting time is not going to get her a raise. What she *really* wants is to qualify for that raise so she can pay her bills, which requires that she increase her productivity.

Police arrest a protester for breaking a window. In the interrogation, the protester tells police he never set out to vandalize an innocent person's property, but his emotions ran high in the excitement of the moment, propelling him to do something he didn't really want to do. He just wanted to be heard.

In each example above, one of the Six Dimensions of Desire was left unbridled or slid too far in one direction, obscuring long-term or more valuable goals in favor of a less meaningful goal. What we *think* we want right now can prevent us from achieving what we really want in the future.

**Why don't we see the reality of our wants and their subsequent tradeoffs?** Wants are comparable to our own breathing; the respiratory process happens so naturally that it goes undetected until someone points it out. Just like breathing, the act of wanting happens constantly in the background. We just don't always recognize it.

When we conscientiously set a goal, we typically analyze the broader implications and tradeoffs required to achieve that goal. However, when we are in an upside-down state of being, we are often blind to the negative effects and unintended consequences of our wants. It's almost as if the upside-down condition equates to looking through a paper towel tube that narrows our focus and removes awareness of our surroundings. From the young child who indiscriminately chases a ball into the street to the person with a drinking problem who irresistibly chases the bottle, neither one is *fully* comprehending in the moment that their seemingly irrepressible wants are leading them into danger.[8] Whether or not the issue is lack of discipline or lack of knowledge, the result reveals the same tradeoff. This is not condemnatory to either the child or the person struggling with a drinking problem, but rather demonstrates how the top segment of the upside-down model inhibits our view. When the figurative ball or the bottle clouds our vision, other aspirations can become obstructed, rendering them practically invisible.

As we progress through the subsequent segments of the upside-down pyramid, we see how feeling, thinking, and behaving in upside-down ways make it increasingly difficult to see things as they really are.

We exchange our more desirable objectives for our impetuous wants—and yet we pretend those tradeoffs don't exist. These concessions are an insidious reality we often ignore or fail to acknowledge as we make regrettable choices.[9] Such examples could include when we want to lose thirty pounds, but we delay our goal with a double-deluxe bacon cheeseburger (toss in fries and a shake). Perhaps an opportunity presents itself at work, but we ignore a previously made commitment and accept the new project, causing delays with the first one. We want to retire at fifty but fall for the new Land Rover purchased with a loan exceeding our budget. We want to move up the corporate ladder, but that goal becomes compromised when we arrive at the office late and attend important meetings unprepared.

The conflicted list of tradeoffs goes on and on. We play this game of give and take every day. While it's one thing to change our goals deliberately and thoughtfully, it's quite another if we don't fully consider the tradeoffs we are making. Reality implicates us when we discover the valuable desires that we dreamed about have morphed into a nightmare because we inadvertently substituted them for impulsive wants.

**How do selfish wants affect relationships?** When we begin a friendship, we are generally mindful and considerate of the other person, striving to enhance their happiness. This attention fosters positive, genuine working relationships. However, as time goes by, if one of us in the relationship becomes focused on our *own* wants and ignores the other person's desires, that relationship usually begins to decay. Of course, it's essential to attend to individual needs, provide self-care, or defend our own values. The point is that our degree of selfishness or selflessness can make a difference.

Selfish, amoral, apathetic, or impatient wanting can lead to feeling upside down. These feelings signal a need for honest and careful evaluation of those wants and their consequences on relationships. When we pursue goals in conflict with those around us, we may or may not diminish what we ultimately want.

In 1938, researchers at Harvard began their work on a generational study about adult development.[10] The endeavor commenced with 268 sophomores and subsequently expanded to more than 1300 of their descendants. For eighty years, researchers identified the participants' health trends and their successes or failures in both their careers and marriages.

Professor of Psychiatry at Harvard Medical School Robert Waldinger (who directed the study) said, "The surprising finding is that our relationships and how happy we are in our relationships has a powerful influence on our health. Taking care of your body is important but tending to your relationships is a form of self-care too."

Conclusions from the study include:

- Close relationships, more than money or fame, are what keep people happy throughout their lives.

- Meaningful relationships delay mental and physical decline.

- Satisfying relationships are better predictors of long and happy lives than social class, intelligence, or even genetics.

The study found that those who maintained close relationships lived longer and were happier, while the lonely and unhappy often died earlier. "Loneliness kills," Waldinger said. "It's as powerful as smoking or alcoholism."

Health and longevity rely on meaningful relationships. Thus, harmonizing our wants with and considering the needs of others lead to less conflict and more peace, resulting in lasting happiness.

**Why do wants potentially cause contention?** Slack's former CEO, Stewart Butterfield, identified a problem with the post-COVID, return-to-office policy: "People don't *want* to be told what to do."[11] We despise it when someone issues a mandate, especially when it is contrary to our beliefs. *We want what we want, and we don't want someone telling us how to live our lives.*[12]

So, while one group wants the right to choose; the other wants the right to protect life. Some want to use traditional gender pronouns while others want more variety. Many want to own guns while others want to abolish them. These are three politically contentious wants! The list of smaller, interpersonal conflicts is even longer.

*Politics* refers to the establishment of laws that govern the behaviors of the people in a community. Politicians argue against each other because they don't *want* to be told what to do or have rules imposed upon them by the dictates of another party. If taken too far in either direction, to the left or to the right, people rebel. Wants explain why politics and religion should be scrupulously avoided at dinner.

---

## We want what we want, and we don't always want what others want.

---

Political dialogs move quickly from casual conversations to high stakes emotional controversy, then irrational statements, and illogical arguments. Both sides feel upside down and powerless to persuade the other. This explains why government is often ineffective. Politicians argue, debate, filibuster, overturn, veto, and attempt to impeach each other, all to no avail. Billions of taxpayer dollars are spent with little to show except a hopelessly divided society. Damn that invisible four-letter word!

**What is the bottom line?** An unregulated want equates to the invisible four-letter word because it often drives us in ways we can't see. When too many impulsive, self-serving, impatient, worthless, chaotic, or otherwise undisciplined wants saturate our lives, they impede our vision and can leave us feeling upside down. Wants manifest themselves in a variety of ways, including verbal and non-verbal responses. We often satisfy immediate wants at the expense of our long-term desires. Selfish wants can create conflict and corrode long-lasting relationships, deflating our happiness. Contentious arguing over wants leads to ineffectiveness and useless divisiveness.

Wants on their own are not necessarily a bad thing. We may have good wants or bad wants. The awareness of our wants enables us to evaluate and regulate them to positive results. The upside-down pyramid addresses what happens when our unrecognized wants get the best of us;

acknowledging them leads to acting more intentionally and having greater control over personal choices and actions.[13]

## Connecting the Principles

Consider your own personal conflict experience relative to the principles of invisible wants, the tradeoff of wants, and wants causing contention:

- Is your want preventing you from getting what you really desire? If so, in what ways?

- If you're dealing with an inner conflict, clearly identify both sides of the conflict and identify which one leads you to what you really want.

- What are other people telling you about your want? Are they seeing things you might not be seeing? Describe them.

- Look back at the Six Dimensions of Desire and describe the position of each slider and why you position it that way. Could adjustments help improve the conflict?

## Segment 2. Negative Emotions

When we have a want, we *feel a need* for something,[14] and if we don't get what we want, we typically become emotional.[15] The internal act of wanting can curiously morph into negative feelings such as anxiousness, anger, or depression. *Desire* the verb (to wish for, long for, or want) becomes *desire* the noun (a feeling, passion, or emotional state). The stronger our wants, the more extreme the corresponding emotions. Whether we like it or not, wants affect our emotions in both good and bad ways.[16]

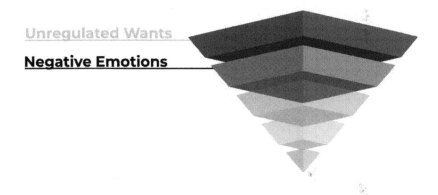

We know what happens when you take a toy away from a small child: they throw a fit! They want the toy; you take it from them, and that unleashes a negative emotional response.

When we don't get what we want, or if we're handed something we don't want (like a speeding ticket), negative emotions naturally emanate from within us—sometimes like a faucet drip and other times like a volcanic eruption if left unchecked.[17]

**How can undetected negative emotions emerge?** Negative emotional responses can unexpectedly leap out of us when we don't get what we want. Bentley's story illustrates the speed at which this can happen.

As he drove his son to school, Bentley was cut off by another driver (which he didn't want), so he angrily flipped the bird and yelled a few obscenities. Speeding up to chase the other driver in a fit of road rage, Bentley was quickly interrupted by his five-year-old son in the back seat who was parroting his filthy language and gestures. Bentley's son snapped him back into the reality. He had inadvertently allowed a moment of negative emotion to alter his typical behavior.

When we feel upside down, it is difficult to detect how our wants are connected to our emotions. Essentially, we are blind to the cause of our passionate reactions the same way that we are blind to our wants. The more intense our wants are, the greater our emotional attachment to them, both positive and negative. If you don't care about winning a game, you are likely to blow it off with a casual shrug. If you're in the championship round because you've worked hard for that achievement, and then you lose, your emotional response will be drastically different.

The English word *upset* perfectly describes this emotional state. Another meaning of the word *upset* is to overturn or to turn upside down.[18] In sports or politics, if the person or team that is expected to win loses, the result is called an "upset." When an upset happens, emotional reactions (both positive and negative) often make the headlines.[19]

Have you ever been out to dinner with a group of people where one very opinionated person in the party did not get exactly what they wanted with their order? On one occasion, a hungry friend of mine emotionally expressed to the server his dissatisfaction with an overdone steak, which wasn't cooked how he wanted. His outburst was embarrassing. After his overzealous tirade, he settled down and casually returned to our conversation in a dignified manner—as if nothing had happened. This incident indicated to me that he could regulate his emotions when he wanted to, but when he didn't get what he wanted, he treated the server disrespectfully and leveraged those negative emotions to get his way. Unfortunately, his dinner companions were mortified as they saw his behavior contradict his typical demeanor.

The wise Roman philosopher Seneca noted, "Anger, if not restrained, is frequently more hurtful to us than the injury that provokes it."[20] Seneca's quotation makes two prominent points. First, anger hurts us more than the person to whom it is directed. And second, we can control our anger to prevent injury. Wisdom prevails when we learn to first recognize and then regulate our negative emotions before they escalate into more serious conflict.

Indeed, we can regulate rising emotions by consciously adjusting the sliders of the Six Dimensions of Desire. We can decide to be independent of negativity in the face of unmet expectations—if we *want* to.

**How does our emotional state affect us?** No one likes to be around an angry person. Negative emotions curtail openness, awareness of reality, and the ability to learn, grow, and work peacefully with others. Negativity temporarily impairs our problem-solving skills, narrows our perspective, diminishes our capacity to overcome opposition, and suppresses our ability to cope with everyday difficulties.[21]

At the turn of the century, neuroscientist Antonio Damasio reported a groundbreaking discovery about how emotions affect the human brain.[22] Damasio studied people with brain damage in the prefrontal cortex, as well as patients with injuries involving the amygdala—the brain center for emotional response.

For the most part, people in the study with a damaged amygdala seemed normal to the outside world, but internally they were unable to feel emotions. Interestingly, all the people in the Damasio study had something peculiar in common: they couldn't make decisions. Patients could describe what they should do in logical terms but found it difficult to make even simple decisions, including things as easy as choosing what to eat. With no emotional guide, the test subjects were unable to problem solve.

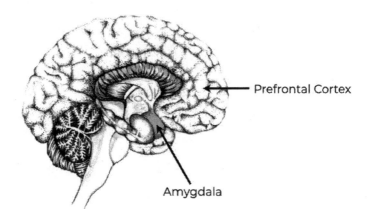

Damasio's research revealed that the amygdala must function properly to help us make even the simplest decisions. If the amygdala succumbs to the influence of negative emotions, then decisions tend to skew toward those negative emotions. But if the brain is governed by positive emotions, choices are more influenced by the larger area of the brain that is responsible for higher-level cognitive processing—the prefrontal cortex. This region of the brain specifically governs the critical thinking skills necessary to make logical connections.

Damasio discovered why even basic decision processes are hampered by negative emotions. In healthy individuals, the prefrontal cortex and amygdala work together to balance and regulate emotional and logical responses. If we encounter a situation of stress, our brain can react quickly with a flood of emotion, causing the amygdala to release cortisol, a stress hormone. Too much unregulated emotion can overwhelm the cognitive control of the prefrontal cortex, preventing full use of our logical reasoning.

Psychologists call this either an "amygdala hijack" or "emotional hijacking," which is commonly described as the human fight-or-flight reaction to stress.[23]

In other words, during a burst of negative emotions (sad, mad, scared), the amygdala "hijacks" our ability to think rationally. When the brain prompts the release of cortisol, it becomes increasingly harder to solve problems or concentrate. This process takes a toll on rationality, and we may not recover our original level of cognitive function for several hours.[24]

This amygdala response explains but does not justify Bentley's emotional outburst. When he was suddenly cut off by another driver who nearly caused an accident, his brain perceived the event as a threat to his safety, triggering a fight response. Bentley's brain stopped relying on logic, and he immediately felt intense anger. He retaliated by yelling at the other driver, flinging a rude gesture, and proceeding to chase him down. These actions were dangerous and irrational, especially with a five-year-old in the back seat. In Bentley's scenario, his emotions "hijacked" the rational thinking part of his brain, causing him to react emotionally without considering the potential consequences of his actions.

Our ability to make decisions relies on emotions, but when we let them control us, we tend to make poor decisions that lead to disappointment or regret. To prevent dreadful responses from happening, we must learn to recognize our emotions in that short but critical window of time before they escape—which is the crux of what regulation means and a primary focus of this book.

**What type of negative emotions emerge from unregulated wants?** Gloria Willcox, a licensed clinical psychologist, created a graphic depiction of emotions that naturally occur when a person does not get what they want.[25] She entitled it "The Feeling Wheel" (shown below).[26] Designed to aid people in recognizing and communicating their feelings,

Willcox labeled primary sections with the names of fundamental feelings, such as mad, sad, or scared. The outer rings contain more refined names of associated feelings that relate to the primary ones.

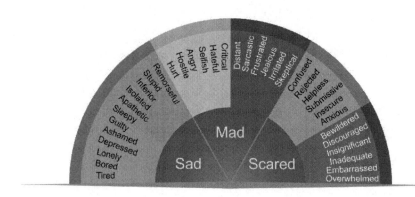

The negative half of The Feeling Wheel portrays the unfavorable emotions we experience when we are feeling upside down—which we all have from time to time. You can test them by saying, "When I don't get what I want, I feel ____."

Awareness of our negative emotions can act as a smoke alarm to alert us that we are moving toward an upside-down state. Disregarding our emotional response to our wants is like disconnecting the batteries in our smoke alarm. You can do it, but it is risky and can be dangerous.

Some negative emotions are subtle and difficult to detect. Others are privately concealed and carefully cloaked. Each has its own set of underlying problems and associated negative outcomes. For example, boredom and loneliness can lead to making poor choices as much as anger.

The Feeling Wheel covers the general spectrum of negative emotions but is not an all-inclusive list. One emotion not listed in The Feeling Wheel that deserves special attention is "offended." To be offended is to feel irritation, anger, or resentment toward another person. Offensive words and actions happen to all of us. As imperfect humans, we hurt each other both intentionally and unintentionally.

Feeling offended could be placed in several positions on this negative half of the feeling wheel. We might overlay it on the Sad-Depressed-Inferior slice, or it could be situated in the Mad-Angry-Frustrated segment or possibly in the Scared-Rejected-Discouraged portion. Feeling offended covers a wide range of negative emotions and should not be left unattended to run wild.

The Western colonizer Brigham Young observed, "He who takes offense when no offense is intended is a fool, and he who takes offense when offense is intended is a greater fool." As a man who encountered many snakes in his lifetime, he then explained that there are two courses of action to follow when one is bitten by a rattlesnake. One may, in anger, fear, or vengeance, pursue the creature and kill it. Or one may make full haste to get the venom out of their system. If we pursue the latter course we may likely survive, but if we attempt to follow the former, we may not be around long enough to finish it.[27]

---

We can decide to be independent of negativity in the face of unmet expectations—if we *want* to.

---

Quite often, when we are feeling upside down and offended by the snakes in our lives, we cultivate (by our own choice) negative emotions that can do more harm than good.[28] Applying a little forgiveness before succumbing to an offense wisely deflects negative emotions.[29]

**What is the bottom line?** When we don't get what we want, we often become emotional. And like an impetuous child, we don't always detect the relationship between our wants and our negative emotions. Negative emotions hurt both us and those around us because they temporarily impair problem-solving skills and restrict our perspective.

Upside-down feelings occur when the emotional response to our wants goes unchecked, decreasing our ability to make a logical, conscientious choice (emotional hijack). As we become aware of our emotions, we can use that consciousness as an early warning system to alert ourselves of an impending upside-down state. This awareness becomes a signal for us to analyze our wants critically and alter our emotions accordingly.

## Connecting the Principles

Briefly describe the emotions you feel from your personal conflict experience:

- What emotions from The Feeling Wheel do you find the most appropriate for your situation?

- Why do you think you feel this way?

- If you have affixed blame to someone or something else for how you feel, how might you correct that?

- How are your emotions affecting your thinking process, and are they possibly preventing you from solving this conflict logically?

## Segment 3. Irrational Conclusions

The third segment in the upside-down pyramid describes where our thoughts go if we fail to regulate our emotions. As described in segment 2, when we don't get what we want, uncontrolled emotions can obstruct the logical thinking process, resulting in hasty and irrational conclusions; irrationality, prejudice, and belief bias are all forms of restricted thinking that can lead to false assumptions.[30]

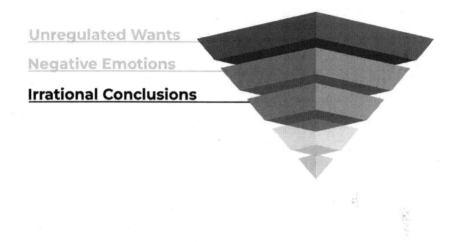

### How do negative emotions lead to irrational conclusions?

Irrational conclusions stemming from negative emotions pretend to be grounded in evidence, facts, and/or common sense. This connection was outlined by psychologist Daniel Goleman in his 1995 book, *Emotional Intelligence: Why It Can Matter More Than IQ*.[31] Goleman coined the "emotional hijacking" term to illustrate that although we have evolved as humans, we retain an ancient structure in our brain designed to respond swiftly to threats. While this response system protected us from danger, in our modern environment it can interfere with our reactions. What used to be a positive response to preserve life while fighting a saber-toothed tiger translates to a negative approach when dealing with our coworkers, boss, or spouse.

Consider the conflict experience you wrote at the beginning of the chapter. What happened inside your head when you did not get what you wanted? Chances are, your mind began spinning with all sorts of ideas, rational and irrational. If you became irrational, how long did that last before you snapped out of it? Were you emotionally hijacked for an hour, or a day, or a week? If you controlled your reactive emotions and didn't become irrational, how did you stop that negative process?

Can you remember a time when you lay awake in bed, your mind turning and twisting over an argument you had with someone close to you? Sleep failed you as you mentally rehearsed how right you were. You struggled to shut off the mental marathon. That awful night passed slowly as you lay emotionally hijacked.

---

When we control our emotions, we harness
the power of cognitive reasoning.

---

*Emotional intelligence* is the capacity to handle interpersonal relationships judiciously and empathetically. When negative emotions flare up and we feel upside down, *emotional unintelligence* replaces emotional intelligence. Negative emotions provoke us to use unintelligent words or say things we don't really mean. Think of two toddlers fighting over a truck; one cries in a fit of rage because his toy has been taken away. Irrationally, he throws himself on the floor and flails wildly, blurting out unbridled expressions like, "I hate you!" He doesn't *really* hate the friend who stole the toy, but in his irrational state of mind, he temporarily is fooled into thinking he does. Unregulated emotions cause logic to fly out the window. If we can't manage our emotions, our critical thinking capability flees from our mind like a herd of zebras from a cheetah.

As adults, we can fall into the same unreasonable trap. At times, we may be tempted to blurt out hurtful words, and on other occasions, we may justify mistreating someone. This is one reason why some people who commit heinous crimes plead not guilty by reason of insanity.[32] They claim irresponsibility for their actions made in a state of high emotion, which is an example of a temporary amygdala hijack.

**How do we snap out of irrational thinking?** One of the best ways to overcome being emotionally hijacked is to ask ourselves *how* we feel. Stopping to recognize and then express feelings re-balances the amygdala with the prefrontal cortex, reestablishing a mental equilibrium. Safely expressing feelings helps us identify the irrational conclusions made during an emotional hijack and then reframe them with factual evidence, which is the basic principle of talk therapy.[33]

Expressing feelings de-escalates emotions
and reconnects us to rational thinking.

Expressions of empathy toward an emotionally hijacked person can also act as a soothing balm to irrationality and help restore feelings of peace. "Agree with thine adversary quickly" is not just good advice from Jesus, but has proven time and again to disarm difficult situations.[34] "I'm sorry about the dent in your car," solicits a better response than "It's not my fault."

While nothing is wrong with expressing emotions (after all we aren't Vulcans from *Star Trek*), we must actively learn to discern and then practice disciplining them accordingly. Emotions themselves are not the root of the problem. The danger lies in allowing our emotions to manipulate our thinking unreasonably to the point that we eventually become pinned under the upside-down pyramid—as Michael honestly confessed in my office. Learning to recognize then regulate our emotions helps us harness the power of cognitive reasoning,[35] which leads to better decision making[36] and more rational solutions.[37]

Thankfully, most episodes of emotional hijacking and irrationality don't usually last very long (for mentally well or disciplined people). But regardless of its duration, an emotional storm can cause damage enough to destroy a relationship like a tornado through a trailer park. More importantly, we typically regret our moments of irrationality. Publius Syrus, a Syrian slave brought to Rome during the time of Julius Caesar, said, "An angry man is again angry with himself when he returns to his reason."[38]

**What are the hidden traps of irrationality?** All of us have times where we speculate or make assumptions about things we don't fully understand or haven't actually verified—which means they may be erroneous. *Erroneous* comes from the Latin word *errare*, meaning to wander.[39] If we make an erroneous assumption, we have wandered away from reason.

An old proverb says, "He that answereth a matter before he heareth it, it is folly and shame unto him."[40] Strong emotions cloud our judgment and lead us to make impulsive, erroneous, or false assumptions. For example, fear can lead us to conclude the worst about a situation, while anger can lead us to make judgments about a person's motives or character. Making false assumptions demonstrates a form of irrational thinking that is not based on reality.[41] A true story illustrates this point.

A tenant called her landlord one day and proclaimed with certainty that the electrical breaker in her apartment had gone bad because it frequently tripped to the OFF position. She demanded that he buy a new breaker and install it immediately because she was afraid of a fire.

The landlord paused to ponder the problem and responded, "Could I ask you to try a few things before I buy a new breaker and install it?"

"Sure," the tenant reluctantly agreed.

"What do you have plugged into the outlet connected to that specific breaker? What appliances stop working when the breaker pops?" he asked.

"There are two things. One is a fish tank heater and the other a microwave," she calmly replied.

He then asked her to unplug both items and flip the breaker to the ON position. When she did, the breaker remained in the ON position.

"That's good," he reassured her.

Next, the landlord asked her to plug the fish tank heater back into the receptacle. The breaker remained in the ON position. Finally, he asked her to plug in the microwave. When she did, the breaker immediately snapped to the OFF position.

"See, I told you the breaker was bad," she proclaimed!

"Actually, that proves that the microwave is faulty," he countered.

"What?!" exclaimed the tenant in defiance. "I can't believe that! I don't have the money for a new microwave. It must be the breaker!"

In the end, a new microwave oven solved what the tenant assumed was an electrical problem.

Some of us are masters at altering the world to fit our wants. When passions run high, false expectations or erroneous beliefs become real. Research reveals that when a person challenges someone's beliefs, those beliefs become stronger simply because of the believer's long-held personal inclination.[42]

In an emotional and irrational state, we flounder in the fountain of false assumptions.[43] Have you ever noticed that during a heated argument, it is nearly impossible to win with verifiable facts? When one person throws out their list of evidence, the other person reinforces their position with equally opposing facts. Who or which list is right? Isn't truth, truth? The answer is yes, but *belief seemingly becomes truth* in an emotional state of irrationality.

---

An upside-down condition makes it
extremely difficult to discern the difference
between facts and opinions.

---

False assumptions can be misleading at their best and harmful at their worst. They tend toward conflict and negative outcomes. Because *we only believe what we WANT to believe,* belief—not truth—creates conflict. To avoid making false assumptions that lead to conflict, we need to recognize our own belief biases and remain open to others' perspectives and experiences.

For example, working in a process engineering role within a manufacturing environment, I have taught many times the benefits of one-piece flow versus batch processing. (The basic difference between batch processing and one-piece flow is in the way production is organized. Batch processing involves processing items in groups or batches, which can lead to inventory and time inefficiencies, while one-piece flow focuses on processing items one at a time, resulting in reduced inventory and quicker response to customer needs.) Each time I teach this principle and run an empirical experiment that visibly demonstrates a *group's* efficiency is greater using one-piece flow than it is using batch processing, someone in the class will say, "Yeah, but I am not as efficient when I use one-piece flow. My personal output is greater when I work in batches."

"Yes, your *personal* efficiency goes down, but the *system's* total throughput increases," I usually respond.

"Yeah, but if *I* am less efficient, then the whole system must be less efficient too," comes the rebuttal.

We go back and forth, arguing about the most efficient system based on our own biases. Only after we run the experiment with conclusive evidence will the skeptics start to change their belief. Even then, people hang on to what they *feel* is true—despite it being disproven—because that is what they want to believe.

Sprinkle in a few negative emotions to reinforce the belief bias, and the critical thinking process remains clouded.[44] When our beliefs are bonded with strong emotions, we justify irrational conclusions as reality—whether true or not. In an upside-down condition, discerning the difference between facts and opinions proves extremely difficult.

**What is the bottom line?** The irrational conclusions segment of the upside-down pyramid describes how emotions suppress our ability to think clearly and work toward a logical explanation. Without rational problem-solving skills, we often resort to prejudiced thinking, speculation, belief biases, false expectations, and assumptions—which lead to erroneous conclusions that tempt us to react in negative ways.

## Connecting the Principles

Reflecting again on your personal conflict experience, consider how your emotions may lead you to irrational thinking:

- When you test the factual evidence supporting or opposing your emotional beliefs, do you discover any discrepancies between your beliefs and reality?

- What would a neutral party say about your conflict?

- Would it make a difference if you switched your point of view with the other person and put yourself in their shoes?

## Segment 4. Reactive Responses

As we continue our descent down the metaphorical upside-down pyramid, we encounter the next segment, which represents the reactive responses we make to our irrational conclusions. These are unregulated physical responses to the false assumptions running amok inside our heads, the stage where thoughts transform into actions, or more accurately, *reactions*. Examples of reactive responses could include knee-jerk reactions such as launching snappy comebacks, rationalizing or embellishing a story, flat-out lying, yelling at someone, running away (avoidance), physical violence, or other conscious or unconscious reactions. A reactive response may be supporting or doing things that you think are right but that infringe on another person's rights.

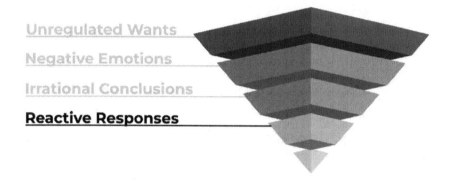

Unregulated Wants
Negative Emotions
Irrational Conclusions
**Reactive Responses**

**How do reactive responses lead to conflict?** The emotionally hijacked mind employs a reactive defense mechanism to manipulate, deny, or distort reality. We often defend our negative emotions and irrational conclusions to prop up our honor and self-esteem.[45] When we find our actions are inconsistent with our ethical standard, we have one of two choices: we can either justify our reactive response or hold ourselves rationally responsible. One choice erodes integrity while the other one fosters it. This doesn't mean that we are necessarily upside down every time we feel anger or frustration. Upside-down behaviors occur when we fail to *regulate* our emotions—thus allowing irrational conclusions to drive a reactive response.

Remember Michael from the beginning of this book? His desire was to be a good employee and provide for his family. But, due to the high stress he felt at work, his financial obligations, and the negative emotional impact those circumstances had on him, he justified heavy drinking in the evenings which conflicted with his goals. He rationalized his want by saying he "needed" alcohol to manage the stress of life. However, that is not what Michael really wanted. Because the realities of heavy drinking prevented him from performing his work responsibilities and meeting his family obligations, Michael essentially traded his life's stability for impulsive wants.

A reactive response also can betray our core values.[46] Abdul-Majeed Alani's story illustrates this point.[47] Alani was an aircraft mechanic who worked for a major airline for over thirty years. On July 17, 2019, he disabled a commercial aircraft's air navigation system by inserting a foam piece into it then using super glue to hold it in place. This plane carried 150 passengers on their flight from Miami to Nassau.

Fortunately, the plane's computer system reported the error, prompting the pilots to abort the take-off and quickly return to the gate. Investigators determined the navigation system had been manually disarmed. Security cameras identified Alani as the culprit.

When questioned, Alani justified his actions by arguing that he was *upset* about contract negotiations. He rationalized that the dispute had affected him financially. He adamantly insisted that his only intent was to delay the flight or cancel it so he could get overtime work. He asserted that his actions were in no way purposeful sabotage designed to cause harm to the plane or the passengers.

Alani's upside-down response is easily discernible from this alarming story. He *wanted* more income, expressed *anger* about the contract negotiations, and became *emotionally hijacked* to the point of *reacting* to his *irrational conclusion* that he would get more overtime by disabling the navigation system—simultaneously justifying his actions with erroneous thinking and dangerous logic.

Is disabling an aircraft the act of a clear-thinking person, or is it indicative of someone experiencing an upside-down condition? What conflicts arose from his reactive response?

Dakota provides another example of a more common reactive response. She wanted a specific day off work for family obligations. Her supervisor could not grant her request because two other, more senior employees already had that week off. Disregarding the denial, she reacted by calling in sick on the day she requested. She got what she wanted—for a while. These self-serving actions eventually turned to distrust, and her employment at the firm ended.

Did Dakota really get what she wanted? Was her steady income a worthwhile tradeoff for avoiding one day at work?

Vengeance is another type of reactive response. Research indicates that individuals experience pleasure while contemplating revenge; however, they rarely feel rewarded afterwards.[48] While vengeance is acting to attain justice, it clearly exposes the irrational conclusion that getting retribution would lead to solving the conflict. Driven by negative and unregulated emotions, the reality of vengeance inhibits our progress toward a positive resolution and traps us in a cycle of anger and bitterness.

Country music star Carrie Underwood brilliantly portrays the symptoms of an upside-down progression in her hit song, "Before He Cheats." Notice how perfectly the lyrics fit the model:

Right now, he's probably slow dancing
With a bleached-blond tramp
And she's probably getting frisky
Right now, he's probably buying
Her some fruity little drink
'Cause she can't shoot whiskey

Right now, he's probably up behind her
With a pool-stick
Showing her how to shoot a combo
And he don't know

I dug my key into the side
Of his pretty little souped-up four-wheel drive
Carved my name into his leather seats
I took a Louisville slugger to both head-lights
I slashed a hole in all four tires
Maybe next time he'll think before he cheats[49]

Wow, that's one upside-down country girl! Of course, she doesn't *want* her boyfriend to be dancing with a "bleached-blond tramp." She *feels fury* just *imagining* it. Notice how he is not slow dancing with another girl; he is *probably* slow dancing. She's not frisky with him, she's *probably* getting frisky. *Probably* demonstrates irrational conclusions from potentially false assumptions. Those "probablys" escalated to a substantial repair bill in *reactive response* damages to her boyfriend's truck.

In the reactive response segment, the emotionally hijacked brain can rationalize anything from minor indiscretions to serious violence. Revenge snowballs into additional acts of injustice.[50] This is when the yelling starts, when the abuse begins, or when the protests turn into riots.[51] It's when shots are fired, bottles are opened, credit cards are swiped, the clothes come off, the leap begins, the road rage happens, the fire starts, the pills are popped, the lies are launched, the rocks are thrown—and many other awful actions and reactions.[52] These impulsive reactions often lead to terrible tradeoffs that stand in stark contrast to what we really want.

**How does timing relate to reactive responses?** The time it takes to go from irrational thoughts to a reactive response is highly variable. This process can happen in a split second or can take weeks or years.

In one example, Philip began feeling remorseful and wanting to make amends to his wife. He sheepishly confessed to her that he had been cheating. Before he could express his regret, she slapped him. In a flash, he slapped her back—yet instantly regretted his unconscious, reactive response.

Sara provides another example. After years of feeling overworked and underpaid, Sara justified skimming off a few dollars for herself from every cash payment she processed. She told herself it was a way of making up for what she *felt* was rightfully hers.

Whether our actions occur in a split second or after years of contemplation, we may find ourselves in serious trouble if we react without thinking through the consequences of our responses.

Countless stories describe how unmet expectations and unrealized wants trigger urgent or impatient reactive responses. However, it is not the time interval that is as important as our ability to recognize our emotions, regulate our response, and then choose an appropriate reaction. Taking time to stop and think through our response often reveals our irrationality, whereas impulsive, impatient reactions magnify conflict.

**What is the bottom line?** False assumptions in our heads can lead to inappropriate physical actions or other reactive responses. The emotionally hijacked mind can rationalize just about anything. We might make offhanded comments, blurt irrational statements, justify our reactions, go to great lengths to prove our personal opinions—or much worse.[53] In this upside-down condition, we often do things we otherwise would not do if our wants were being fulfilled or regulated in healthy ways. In this senseless state, rather than acting with foresight or patience, we are reacting without regard to where those actions lead.

## Connecting the Principles

Reflecting again on your personal conflict experience, evaluate how you are reacting to your situation:

- Do you feel like you have been in control and are acting willfully with a logical presence of mind, or are your responses hasty or impulsive?

- What about the other person? How are they acting or reacting?

## Segment 5. Powerless Position

Notice the size, shape, and location of the last segment in the upside-down pyramid. It is small and insignificant, but its shape is piercing. Like the lowest point in a funnel, a person in this stage of the metaphor has few options. The powerless position segment physically represents what Michael mourned as "being pinned under the point of an upside-down pyramid."

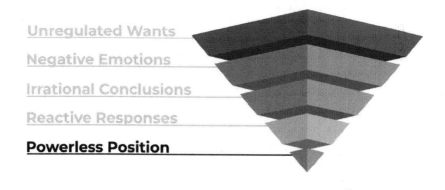

Unregulated Wants

Negative Emotions

Irrational Conclusions

Reactive Responses

**Powerless Position**

**How do we end up in a powerless position?** Finding yourself in a powerless position can be like being caught red-handed in a robbery. You have the money in your hands, and then, click, the lights come on! You got what you wanted, but is it what you *really* wanted? And now you can't put it back. At this point, undoing the damage almost always requires significant effort or pain. A person arrives in a powerless position through a series of unrecognized wants and choices made from unregulated responses that ultimately lead to powerlessness.

Herman Melville's short story "Bartleby, the Scrivener" illustrates this powerlessness. A lawyer who runs a law office on Wall Street begins the tale by explaining that he has known many scriveners (law-copyists) during his career, but none as interesting as Bartleby. The unnamed lawyer has three employees: two scriveners and an assistant.

The lawyer hires Bartleby as his third scrivener. At first, he seems to be a great employee and does what the lawyer asks of him; however, the lawyer's difficulty with Bartleby begins when it is time to proofread his documents. To efficiently check for accuracy, all the employees sit together with copies and read through them aloud. This process is described by the lawyer as being "an indispensable part of a scrivener's business." When Bartleby is asked to participate, he replies, *"I would prefer not to,"* which is another way of saying, "I don't *want* to."

Shocked by this response, the lawyer presses Bartleby, who continues to reply, "I would prefer not to." Exasperated, the lawyer continues the proofreading without Bartleby.

After this, Bartleby declares, "I would prefer not to," every time he is asked to do a task, no matter how small. The lawyer has no idea how to deal with Bartleby's unreasonableness and therefore continues to give in to his manipulation.

One Sunday, the lawyer stops by the office but cannot open the door. Something is wedged in the keyhole. Suddenly, the door unlocks from the inside and out pops Bartleby, who has presumptuously moved into the office!

With Bartleby's unwelcome tenancy in the office, insubordination, and refusal to complete any work, the lawyer decides his only recourse is to move his business to another location. It is not long before the new tenant of the lawyer's office shows up, demanding to know who the heck Bartleby is and why he is still living in the old office. The lawyer claims no responsibility for Bartleby, but the new tenant insists Bartleby is not his problem either and persists until the stymied lawyer agrees to speak with the burdensome Bartleby. He offers suggestions, but Bartleby refuses all offers, simply replying, "I'd not prefer any of them."

Frustrated, the new tenant calls the police to have Bartleby physically removed from the building and taken to a New York jail known as The Tombs. Feeling compassion, the unnamed lawyer visits Bartleby there, where he pays the grub man to provide Bartleby with better food—yet Bartleby stops eating altogether, saying he would "prefer not to dine." At the end of the story, the lawyer shows up and finds Bartleby dead. He exclaims in the epilogue, "Ah, Bartleby! Ah, humanity!"[54]

When we "*prefer not to*" regulate our wants we end up like Bartleby: unhelpful, powerless, and possibly irrelevant. Melville hit the nail on the head with his "Ah, humanity" statement: Bartleby chose to willfully set aside his true desires (what he really wanted) for what he wanted in the moment (to do nothing).

**What happens when we become stuck in powerlessness at the bottom of the upside-down pyramid?** While Bartleby's story generalizes the powerless position in a fictional story, consider this true account of Edward and Elaine Brown.[55] The Browns were both business entrepreneurs; he owned a pest control business while Elaine ran a dental practice. They both took great pride in their careers and were passionate about their success. Over time, feelings of resentment built within them about the amount of money they were paying for taxes. The last thing they wanted was to give thousands of hard-earned dollars to the government. Hostility grew in their minds for years, which germinated into obstinate anger. Negative emotions helped them justify their refusal to pay income taxes. Edward and Elaine rationalized their decision by telling themselves that the government had no right to their money. They stopped disclosing income altogether.

Soon, they were visited by the IRS, which filed judgments with penalties against them. This led to a nine-month, armed standoff with federal law enforcement authorities at their New Hampshire residence.

The Browns were eventually arrested, found guilty by a federal district court jury, and convicted—with additional criminal charges arising from their conduct during the standoff.

Edward and Elaine's story reflects the sequence and consequences of upside-down behaviors. They did not *want* to pay their taxes and were indignant about it. They justified the idea that the government had no right to their money. When they stopped obeying the law, *external forces* removed their freedom to act. Because of their series of upside-down choices, the Browns traded their beautiful home in New Hampshire for separate cells in federal prison—leaving them both powerless!

What makes this account relatable is the fact that no one *wants* to pay taxes, but we do it because we logically understand the consequences of not paying them and acknowledge the benefits taxes provide.

Like a funnel, the downward momentum that occurs at the bottom of the inverted pyramid and the small size of its point illustrates an absence of choices, the limited options and natural consequences of being stuck at the bottom of the powerless position. By controlling our wants and emotions at the top, we can avoid the trap at the bottom and the associated lack of choice that ironically come from not controlling our wants and emotions.[56] In other words, if you don't use your free will wisely, you just might lose it altogether.

Let's not ignore the fact that accidents do happen, and any of us can feel powerless because of another person's careless decisions or cruel actions. That is not the type of powerlessness I am describing. What I am asserting is that the secret to power lies in *how we act on* what happens to us. By controlling how we respond, *we choose a direction that aligns with what we ultimately want in the future, regardless of the situation's origins.* A famously extreme example of this is found in Viktor Frankl's personal experiences documented in his memoir, *A Man's Search for Meaning.*

In everyday scenarios where we are trending upside down, we can end up in a powerless position through our poor reactions. We emotionally position the Six Dimensions of Desire the way we want them adjusted. When the settings are not in harmony with others or create internal dissonance, social pressure may persuade us to point fingers and assign blame for unfulfilled expectations and not getting what we want. Deflecting responsibility creates powerlessness.

To be sure, this isn't a condemnation as much as an acknowledgement that every human inadvertently falls for these traps. When caught in this powerless state, we tend to proclaim, defend, justify, mistakenly believe, or fall prey to false ideas in some form or another.[57] These insidious distortions could include coverups for our wants such as, "You made me do it," "It's not my fault," "I'm a victim," or "I was born this way." These excuses reveal an external locus of control.[58] Giving up responsibility for our circumstances inhibits the likelihood of escaping the pressure-producing, upside-down pyramid. Increasing our recognition helps prevent us from stepping into subtle snares.

By controlling our wants and emotions at the top of the upside-down pyramid, we can avoid the trap at the bottom.

The realities of life dictate that if I am an employee who fails to perform my duties, my boss will let me go. When I am untruthful with a friend, she will stop trusting me. If I'm abusive to someone I love, they are going to leave. In each case, a relationship suffers severe damage. The ability to repair it dramatically diminishes. The damage is done, the honor has been lost, and the ability to choose has been surrendered—resulting in a powerless position difficult to reverse.

**What is the bottom line?** True powerlessness is usually a self-inflicted consequence of unregulated wants. When the upside-down pyramid pins us in a place we don't want to be, it's easy to try to escape responsibility by assigning fault elsewhere. But if we want to break the bondage, we can't continue blaming others, the world, nature, God, our parents, our neighbors, our boss, our genetics, our spouse, the government, the police, the economy, the weather, addiction, peer pressure, a horoscope, or any number of rationalized excuses.

The powerlessness that this segment describes starts from being upside down, and being upside down is rooted in unrecognized and unregulated wants. When we properly recognize our wants for what they are and regulate them accordingly, we can engage our free will to choose a better outcome and restore freedom.

## Connecting the Principles

Let's apply this concept to your personal conflict experience:

- Are you getting—or have you achieved—what you wanted?

- Do you feel like you have more or fewer choices now?

- Where will you go from here?

# Disharmony and Dishonor: Products of the Upside-Down Pyramid

This chapter exposes the natural cause-and-effect relationship between our wants and where they can lead represented by segments of the upside-down pyramid. The natural consequence of unregulated and out-of-harmony wants—in all their complexities and various forms—is dishonor and disrespect.

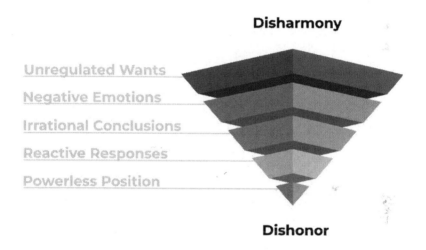

When the Six Dimensions of Desire are positioned badly, then dishonorable feelings develop, either within us or between people; at those times, when we become obsessed with *only* wanting what *we* want, we can feel an absence of honor, respect, and dignity. While it isn't necessarily bad to want different things than others, sometimes we act too selfishly, too intensely, too urgently, too chaotically, and sometimes even immorally. We may even trade what we value most for something of lesser worth, creating internal dissonance.

Remember, disharmony within us and with others increases as we fail to *recognize* and *regulate* the natural struggle that exists between conflicting wants in their various forms, the diverse wants of others, and our responses to those wants. The natural result of disharmony at the top of the upside-down pyramid is dishonor at the bottom of the pyramid.

So, how can you judge whether you are upside-down? First, recognize your wants. Second, pay close attention to your feelings. Whenever you notice negative emotions swelling inside, you might determine if you're feeling upside down by asking yourself these questions:

- Am I feeling discord with others?

- Am I clinging to what I want?

- Am I making excuses by justifying my wants?

- Am I feeling powerless to make changes in my life?

Answering these questions helps us recognize the wants that can create conflicts. Regulating those wants is another matter. Again, being or feeling upside down is not a conviction, nor is it a permanent label or representative of a person's identity—it is a *temporary* state of being. We all feel and act this way at times because our wants try to take over our lives. While these problematic human tendencies and potential conflicts can feel overwhelming, blue skies are in the forecast! This section of the book has been an exploration of the problem, the barrier to achieving what we really want. In the next section, we flip over this metaphorical pyramid to discover a more positive way of responding to our wants.

Section Two

# THE SOLUTION

*Regulated responses to our wants can reduce conflict and promote harmony. As we learn to prioritize and sacrifice less-valuable wants, a sequence of favorable reactions impact our lives and the lives of others in rewarding and positive ways.*

# CHAPTER 5

# HARMONY

*"When you want something, all the universe conspires in helping you to achieve it."*

—Paulo Coelho

The story about Michael in chapter 2 introduced the discovery of the invisible four-letter word. Humbly, Michael admitted that his life was feeling upside down, and he needed to change. He had to find a way to focus on what he *really wanted*. The following excerpt from Michael's journal reveals what he learned about responding proactively when the upside-down pyramid is crushing his chest. In his own words, Michael describes his first week at Delancey Street:

> I remember the first morning clearly. A 6 a.m. wake-up call and we were off to a morning meeting, breakfast, and the day's work. I worked side by side with guys I would never have seen myself with. These guys had done hard jail time most of their lives. San Quentin, LomPoc, Oakland, East L.A.—these were the places they called home. Tattooed from forehead to toe, these were really tough-guy types. Interesting thing, though, is that I came to realize that the choices I had made in my life got me to the same place they were:

Delancey Street. I had gone through the same interview process they did. I was admitted just as they were. I was no different than any one of them.

Sure, the path that I had taken might have been a bit different. Alas, I was there right next to them. Shoulder to shoulder, wiping walls, cleaning bathrooms, vacuuming halls, mopping, scrubbing—you name it—we did it, and we did it all together.

The tack I started to take was a little different. I would try to spin the conversation into a positive, life-changing one. It was a survival mechanism for me. Try to understand—I was miserable. I wanted to leave every second of every waking moment. In order for me to survive, I started talking about how amazing the opportunity was there. I started to speak about how we have the opportunity in each moment to be the best of ourselves, that to do so, we had to look beyond our own suffering and reach into the suffering of others.

One night, before sleep, I was feeling particularly lonely, sad, and tired of my life … which is just crap, because Delancey Street is one of the safest, warmest, most healing places on the planet. I decided that in order for me to stay, I was going to have to do what I was telling everyone else they should do. I would think about someone else for a change. When I woke up the next morning, I would begin to think about the person who was struggling the most, and I would try to spend as much time as I could trying to make their day a little better.

So, I did just that. There was a young guy that had been having difficulty adjusting from institutional life to the beautiful environment we were in. I asked my boss if I could work side by side with the young guy that day, and he said, "Sure." I did everything I could to distract him from the world of pain he thought he was in. I told him really silly jokes that I had remembered my son telling me. He would move off down the hall to clean somewhere else, and I'd be right there with him. I talked about the amazing opportunity we had while there to really make a change. We could go back to our families as different men. All we had to do was to reach out and care, actually care, about the well-being of someone else.[1]

Michael's experience illustrates a powerful principle. When he forgot about himself and focused on others, he subconsciously freed himself from his unstable, chest-crushing, upside-down state of mind.

Likewise, when we harmonize our Six Dimensions of Desire with others, feelings of affinity, unity, and stability change our attitude and behavior in remarkable ways. Jordan Peterson said it more succinctly: "The schism between good and bad is just disunity."[2]

When Michael began looking outward and learned to harmonize his neighbors' needs with his own, his experience at Delancey Street improved.

## The Principle of Harmonious Wants

A choir demonstrates harmony when they sing different notes but complementary tones that are pleasing to the ear. Orchestras and bands take that principle even further: various instruments with drastically different voices, from strings to horns and even drums, integrate their unique sounds and individual flavors to produce gratifying music. One reason why churches have their members sing together is to create a natural and delightful feeling of harmony within the congregation. We sing at birthday parties to give someone a special experience. At sporting events, we sing the national anthem to promote feelings of patriotism and camaraderie. Even the classic seventh inning stretch song, "Take Me Out to the Ball Game!" energizes a crowd and rallies the fans as they "root, root, root for the home team."[3]

Can you imagine a stadium full of people singing different songs? What good would that do? It would be a disjointed mess of madness and chaotic noise. In a harmonious social system, we cannot just sing what we each *want* to sing; we sing *together*, to engender harmony and create a cooperative effort. That said, each person in the figurative stadium can and will have different individual wants and needs, which we must also respect.

Even if you haven't experienced a traffic roundabout, every time you get in your car and drive down the road, the principle of harmonious wants plays out. Respectful drivers, on some level, willingly unite their wants by following the rules of the road. They stay in their lanes, drive the posted speed, stop at traffic lights, and allow pedestrians to cross the road safely. Traffic laws are designed to give each driver what they want—a safe and uneventful arrival to their intended destination.

What would happen if a few people decided that traffic rules were infringing on their personal freedom? What if some people *wanted* to drive on the opposite side of the road—or drive twice the speed limit, or blow through traffic lights regardless of their color? The answer is obvious: there would be chaos, disharmony, and physical carnage. So, to prevent disaster, we willingly harmonize our wants with the rules of the road to get where we are going—while we also work in unity with other drivers.

Cooperation with others doesn't display weakness as some may suppose. Rather, it helps deliver us to our long-term destination. Harmony acts as the progenitor of peace and prosperity. Isn't that what most of us really want?

Despite our differences, we can achieve some level of harmony when we try to support and care for each other while respecting our unique talents and perspectives. When we use kindness, consideration, and respect in our interactions, we all tend to be happier and feel the benefits of a harmonious community.

No one side of a conflict should ever get everything they want (or we end up with totalitarianism). Both sides must make concessions to support the principles and desires we do share. A few examples illustrate this principle.

A flock of migrating birds provides a natural example of individuals acting in harmony. When breaking down a video, frame by frame, scientists have discovered that birds move together perfectly because they work in a democratic system. With the flap of their wings, each bird essentially votes on which direction to go, and as soon as they reach majority consensus, the flock flies in that direction. This process repeats over and over to create a community of individual birds that moves as one body.[4]

In many sports, when a coach calls a play, the entire team subordinates to the plan. Each player willingly contributes to the play as directed and in unison because they honor the authority and wisdom of the coach. If individual players only did what *they* wanted, independent of the coach's direction, the result would be chaos on the field and losses of the game.

---

The magic of harmony lies in our combined power to achieve exponentially more than we ever could alone.

---

Likewise, when we arrive at work each day, seeking to unite ourselves with the goals of our employer, the company honors us with a paycheck. In contrast, direct disharmony between us and our company evaporates honor like an ice cube in the desert heat. The door of honor mutually swings both ways.

Considering and respecting each other as we continually regulate our own wants helps us achieve peace and harmony in our family, in work relationships, and within organizations. Striving to work together using our personal talents and complementary differences—but staying focused on our shared goals—helps to unite rather than divide us.

The synergy of purpose and shared desire to work harmoniously enables exponentially greater results than if we worked alone or without cooperation: We achieve more together than we do alone. Harmony helps us win more games, protect others from dangers, and increase business success.

## The Magic of Harmony

We know that disharmony leads to conflict and dishonor. Conversely, seeking harmony dissipates conflict as we choose to work together peacefully despite our differences. Harmony means honoring and respecting the feelings and wants of those around us, which paradoxically elevates us together. Consider the choir with male and female voices singing various notes at different volumes and intensities. Each individual with a distinct part purposefully blends with the people around them to create something more fantastic than any one of them could create on their own.

How can harmony help us get what we really want? Choosing harmony helps break down the barriers of opposing wants and differing approaches. Even when we can't reconcile our wants with what others want, we can at least agree to disagree in loving ways. Our deepest desires become more attainable when we consider the perspectives and cares of those around us. Reaching our goals feels better when we cooperate and support each other.

Harmony offers multiple benefits such as improved relationships, reduced stress, increased productivity, enhanced creativity, and a healthier mental capacity. Further, choosing to understand with an open heart and mind what others want repels contention and prevents minor situations from becoming serious battles.

Harmonizing our wants also means blending our timing with goals and relationships, tempering our passions, regulating our own warring wants, and carefully comparing and valuing how those wants correlate with what we really find worthwhile. The discipline we use to harmonize our objectives helps us keep wants in check, using our values and ethical standards to guide our choices while we consider the needs of others.

It may seem oversimplified, but it all comes down to what we *really* want in the long term and in each situation. Do we *really* want harmony? Or are we insistent that we only have things our way? Each of us must answer these questions for ourselves and then find the discipline to conscientiously make a choice that hopefully leads to a productive end result and eventual peace.

The magic of harmony lies in our combined power to achieve exponentially more than we ever could alone—just like the beauty of a chorus far surpasses a single voice.

# CHAPTER 6

# THE UPRIGHT PYRAMID

*"Mastering others is strength. Mastering*
*yourself is true power."*

—Tao Te Ching

Imagine yourself now standing on top of the Great Pyramid of Giza. With an unobstructed, 360-degree panorama of the world, the view is magnificent, and you can see for miles! Looking closer, you notice every course of stone from the top to the bottom of the pyramid, and you marvel at how each block fits together, carefully crafted to support the entire structure. This vantage point gives you a more accurate view of reality. Additionally, the base of this pyramid stands strong, stable, and balanced.

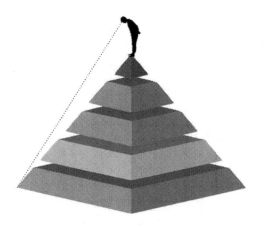

# The Upright Pyramid Sequence

As we methodically position our wants like stones on a physical pyramid and align them with the desires we value most, we strengthen our relationships and stabilize our goals. The pyramids of Egypt have existed for centuries because of their architecture and craftsmanship. Likewise, as we carefully craft our wants, a durable and confident dignity protects us from life's inevitable turmoil. This is not to say that regulating our wants solves every problem, but that most daily dilemmas and common conflicts can be successfully navigated or solved in peaceful and positive ways by applying the principles in this book.

I personally have witnessed colleagues exhibit calm, reassuring, demeanors when the storms of life pounded on them. The potential negativity of unfulfilled wants produced fewer detrimental effects on them because of their solid foundation. Resilient emotional strength over time endows the upright person with honor and respect. I have seen these same people reach out to friends as a stabilizing force, even as they experienced tremors in their own lives. These rare, natural leaders have nothing to prove to the world because they know that time testifies of their consistency, dependability, and integrity—just like the unshakable pyramids of Egypt.

---

Wants worth pursuing are carefully measured, intentionally disciplined, and thoughtfully organized.

---

How can we achieve such self-mastery? The upright pyramid contains five fundamental segments similar to the upside-down pyramid but opposite in nature, revealing the results of positive choices. These include:

1. Regulated Wants

2. Positive Emotions

3. Rational Conclusions

4. Proactive Actions

5. Powerful Position

## Segment 1. Regulated Wants

The first principle of the upright pyramid also contains wants, but these desires are regulated and intentional. The difference between the upside-down (Unregulated Wants) segment and the upright (Regulated Wants) segment is like comparing the difference between a thoughtfully furnished home and one full of hoarded items.

## Regulated Wants

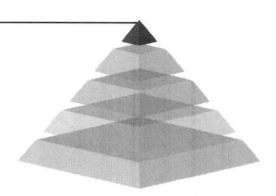

The wants at the top of both pyramids are inseparably connected to their foundations because every want leads to a somewhat predictable conclusion. This truth reveals why regulating our wants is so crucial. As we explored at the outset, our multidimensional desires are layered in complexities. We all actively want and pursue wants. The small capstone of the upright pyramid represents our sincerest wants, our greatest desires, and loftiest goals that are thoughtfully controlled and managed within the Six Dimensions of Desire. Our character choices form our base of ethics. These good wants reflect our bottom-line values.

Pointing upward and outward, the shape and direction of the wants in the upright pyramid illustrate a selflessness that regards others' needs with an attitude of caring. In contrast, unbridled wants that are all-consuming (like unhealthy obsessions) point downward and inward.

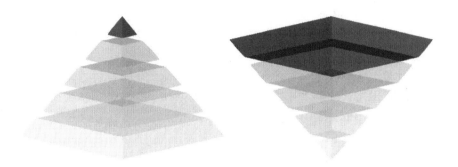

Even though the Regulated Wants segment looks small, it includes our most substantial goals, the things we really want. This small segment doesn't contain just any impetuous or wily want that attractively walks through the door. Its high price and exclusivity demand that we make choices and set priorities.

Have you known a person who doesn't seem to want much, in terms of things, versus a person who appears always to be wanting? A person who is typically in an upright mindset focuses on *who* they are and on doing good things instead of *what* they don't have and pursuing what they want next.

The Roman philosopher Seneca is said to have summed it up this way, "How few are our real wants! and how easy it is to satisfy them! Our imaginary ones are boundless and insatiable."[1]

### How do we evaluate our wants and choose the right ones?

Knowing that we have the inherent power of choice and the responsibility to regulate our desires, each of us must choose the ethical standards that guide our decisions. However, we must respect and find harmony with the alternative beliefs and standards of those around us, despite how different they may be from our own.

Being upright does *not* mean we cast away every personal desire or do anything everyone else wants us to do regardless of our own beliefs. It does mean we identify our values without being dissuaded by others' demands or opposing standards. Balanced, upright wants are carefully measured, intentionally disciplined, and thoughtfully organized. They require the deliberate pursuit of our deepest desires, not the abdication of all desire. That said, consideration of others must always play into *how* we go about pursuing our upright wants. Respect must dominate our relationships, even when our standards and lifestyles dramatically differ from others. With respect as our standard, we can use discipline to respond appropriately to the conflicts inherent in societies' diverse wants. This discipline defines the regulation of our wants.

So, which wants are right and which ones are wrong?

For the sake of illustration, I share my own criteria for determining if what I want is right or appropriate for me. First and foremost, as a believer in the Judeo/Christian God, I ask myself, *Are my wants in harmony with His commandments?* When it comes to wanting, we cannot each be our own moral authority; there must be some higher power to suppress the chaos that would result from each of us egocentrically wanting only what *we* want. God is the ultimate authority with whom I choose to align my wants. He is at the top of my pyramid.

Once I have passed my wants through that primary filter, then I ask three other questions. Does my want or my response to a want:

- Lead to lasting joy for me and others whom I care about?

- Increase my and others' opportunities to make future choices?

- Elevate others, empowering them and me to become better?

Sometimes the answer to these questions is that I need to temporarily sacrifice what I want now to get what I really want later. For example, I love backpacking, but on the weekend of my wife's birthday, I choose to sacrifice backpacking to stay home so she feels loved. That regulation of wants allows me the freedom to go backpacking on other less important weekends without harming our relationship.

---

We enhance relationships when we offer
something *we want* to someone
who is *in want.*

---

Consider John Robert Fox, a United States artillery officer who was serving in Italy during the Second World War. In December 1944, Fox was instructed to stay in the village of Sommocolonia while his unit retreated from the Nazi invasion. He secured himself advantageously on the second floor of an abandoned house to relay the enemy's position. After a few successful strikes, Fox ordered the shelling to his exact location because the Nazis had infiltrated the building where he hid. The gunner refused, but the order came again when Fox demanded, "Fire it! There's more of them than there are us." After the salvo ended and the troops retook the city, Fox's body was found amid one-hundred dead German soldiers.[2]

Less fatal and more common are the stories of thousands of altruistic people who donate kidneys to strangers. Take for instance Dylan Matthews, who was one of over 5,600 people in 2016 to provide a kidney for someone he did not know. Matthews remarked, "I kept coming back again to the concept that if you have the opportunity to help someone at a low cost for yourself, you should go for it."[3]

Whether it is a low cost or the ultimate cost, one way to become more right-sided may be to offer willingly something *you want* to help someone who is *in want*. For example, when I employ the skills of regulating my wants wisely and making sacrifices when necessary, I almost always end up with what I really want. Other situations may be completely different and might require that you assert your position to preserve your integrity. There may be some situations where surrendering what you want could compromise your choices or place you in peril (such as physical danger). Considering your circumstances and where each choice leads ultimately provides the direction for where to go.

Consciously regulating what we truly want is the essence of wisdom. By contrast, we become a servant to our wants when they control us.

Dr. Seuss penned:

You have brains in your head,
You have feet in your shoes,
You can steer yourself in any direction you choose. [4]

**What distracts us from our true wants?** Distractions come in various forms and derail us in sneaky ways. The fewer wants you have, the fewer conflicts with your real wants you'll encounter. More wants equal more opportunities for both external and internal conflicts to arise. Here is an everyday example to which most everyone can relate: You are sitting in a theater enjoying a movie, and you have no other wants. Life is good. As soon as you get a hankering for some popcorn and a soda, the conflict begins. Do you stay in the theater, or do you go get the snacks? You really want the popcorn and justify that it will only take a minute or two. But then you are met with a really long line at the concession bar. You justify that you are already committed to the popcorn. As you return to the movie, the audience is roaring with laughter—you obviously missed something good.

Now you're mad. You begin consuming the popcorn and soda. Thirty minutes later, you need to go to the bathroom! You can't believe it. The show is reaching a plot point you don't want to miss, but your bladder is about to explode. None of these conflicts would have existed had you kept your desire to see the movie uncluttered by extra or disruptive wants.

While this simple example seems trite compared to our deepest desires described earlier, it illustrates that when we choose to control our wants, our wants cannot control us. Simplifying our wants helps us keep them in check.

When we learn to focus and prioritize a few beneficial wants, we unencumber our lives. Socrates taught, "The fewer our wants, the nearer we resemble the gods."[5]

Removing distractions from what we really want entails culling lesser valued wants by sacrificing them while simultaneously elevating the greater ones. This type of regulation helps us achieve what we really want.

**How do we seek good wants but sometimes do it the wrong way?** Sometimes we unintentionally sabotage our own efforts to get what we really want by going about it in the wrong way. One example of this happens when we force our will or timing on others, mistakenly believing it will get us what we want. For example, I have a daughter who loved her cat. When she was young, she wanted to hold it constantly, but sometimes the cat did not want to be held. She would struggle and fight with the cat just to keep it on her lap, so the cat would leap to freedom at the slightest chance. Sometimes my wife would take the same cat to an assisted living community and let a senior friend of ours, Daisy, hold the cat for several hours. Daisy never forced the cat to stay on her lap, yet it would lie there all afternoon, soaking up Daisy's love.

My daughter forced her wants on the cat, which repelled it from her. On the other hand, Daisy gently loved the cat, which included giving it freedom. This small difference caused the feisty feline to endear itself to Daisy, and it rarely left her lap.

The experience of probate lawyers illustrates using the wrong means to an end, which also shows the difference between the two pyramid metaphors. More families argue over the terms of wills and estates than the number who simply accept them as they are written.[6] Family members battle because they want material goods, and they want their fair share. They fight long and hard, spending so much money on additional legal fees that they often end up with less than if they had simply accepted the terms of the will as it was originally drafted.

Wanting "their fair share" unintentionally ends up causing the lawyers to get the larger share of the estate. Worst of all, this type of conflict destroys precious family relationships.

### How can considering others' wants enrich relationships?
When we wisely follow the counsel to "Do to others as you would have them do to you," selflessness enlarges our capacity to make meaningful contributions at home, in organizational teams, and in our communities.[7] Balancing our wants with the wants of those around us communicates to others that we care. At the top of the upright pyramid, wants are borne of love, giving, and service. This is the major paradigm shift between the upright and the upside-down pyramids.

Relationships endure when built on a foundation where both people consider each other's wants. In contrast, relationships break down when we think *our* wants are the most important.[8] Selfish marital relationships are more likely to be filled with contempt and end in divorce.[9] On the flip side, numerous studies verify that generosity in marriage is highly correlated with marital satisfaction.[10]

The transition from wanting what *we* want to wanting what others want, or even what our *future selves* want, is not always easy but possible. This conversion requires consideration, sacrifice, and deference. Applying these generous tactics can feel emotionally difficult, but the probability of successfully navigating this transition increases when we recognize that we are not forced, but rather we choose to harmonize our wants with what other people want.

---

Relationships endure when built on a foundation where both people consider each other's wants.

---

Consider the husband who comes home after a stressful day at work. He enters the house and greets his wife with an affectionate kiss. Before he can get a word out, she unloads on him the difficulties of her day. If he is practicing the upright methodology, he puts aside some of his desires (to sit down, scroll through his phone, and unwind) and genuinely listens to his wife's hardships. Considerately and thoughtfully, he suspends his wants for his wife's wants. No real sacrifice occurs here because what he is doing helps him progress toward what he ultimately wants: a happy wife and a fulfilling marriage.

Likewise, his wife must be mindful of her husband's day at work, his feelings, and his needs so that she is not always the one wanting. In any successful marriage, both spouses must learn to defer equally to each other's wants.

When we establish these types of habits and want the positive feelings that are associated with them, we begin to take pleasure in satisfying other people's wants. Compassion, empathy, and other expressions of love prove the most powerful forces in the universe.

When we truly love someone, we want the very best things for them, even if we do not or cannot want exactly what they want. For example, imagine that you have a child who wants to pursue a lifestyle with which you disagree. You love that child enough to respect their choice (an upright response), despite wanting the child to follow a different path that you feel fits with your own desires. Alternatively, a harsh or unloving reaction to their wants could set off an upside-down scenario.

Potential conflicts like this highlight the importance of prioritizing our wants. Thus, if our deepest desire is to maintain our relationship with the child, then that want supersedes the tendency or impulse to contend with the child's choice.

In most circumstances, we enrich our relationships when we balance our wants relative to others' wants, respect their choices even when they oppose ours, and prioritize our own dimensions of desire accordingly. These forms of consideration and respect demonstrate our care for others and build trust within our relationships.

**What is the bottom line?** The capstone of the upright pyramid represents the regulation of the invisible four-letter word. Specifically, it characterizes what we *really want*. This segment symbolizes our deepest desires, our life's strategic goals and values, our most crucial wants that drive us forward, and those desires governing the lesser wants that try to disrupt us every day. It also illustrates who we want to be. As we learn to prioritize and regulate our wants, less meaningful wants usually fade away.

What we want right now, how intensely we want, and the price we will pay for those desires inevitably influence our future. Maintaining respect and patience in our pursuit of what we really want helps us harmonize our wants with others and builds meaningful relationships. Disciplining and focusing our wants empower us to achieve our most important desires, seek harmony along the way, and cultivate long-lasting relationships.

## Connecting the Principles

Think about your personal conflict experience:

- What are your right-sided wants—the things you really want —and how do they relate to the conflict?

- What distractions may be preventing you from getting what you truly want?

- What sacrifices might you need to make to prioritize your wants and align them with your values?

- How do your right-sided wants affect your relationships within this conflict?

## Segment 2. Positive Emotions

As illustrated in the upside-down model, wants are inseparably connected with our emotions. Remember how negative emotions can seize control of our brains, hijacking our ability to think rationally? In contrast, positive emotions flow freely when we attain what we want most.

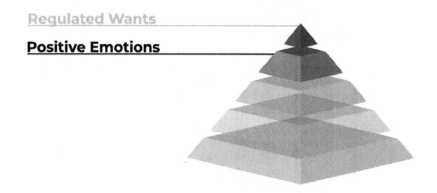

Regulated Wants

**Positive Emotions**

For example, when a child wants ice cream and the parent obliges, happiness fills their little soul. Or think of the adult audience members on the popular TV game show, The Price is Right. When a person's name is called to "Come on down!" they jump for joy, scream with jubilations, and even cry in delight at the sound of their own name—which is exactly what they want!

Paradoxically, positive emotions also can come from sacrificing less important wants to help someone else. Have you ever stopped what you were doing to help someone in need? Did you ever give money to someone who was struggling financially? Have you ever stayed late at work to satisfy a customer's request? Surrendering your wants to someone or something else willingly or selflessly (in a reasonable situation) naturally leads to positive emotions.[11] James Keller affirmed, "A candle loses nothing by lighting another candle."

**What are the physical effects of positive emotions?** Service to others, a simple form of generosity, benefits our physical and mental health by contributing to positive feelings. "Volunteering moves people into the present and distracts the mind from the stresses and problems of the self," said Dr. Stephen G. Post, of the Stony Brook University School of Medicine in New York. "Many studies show that one of the best ways to deal with the hardships in life is not to just center on yourself, but to take the opportunity to engage in simple acts of kindness."[12]

Trevor Norton, an assistant professor at the Harvard Business School, conducted a series of studies that revealed people are generally happier when they spend money on others rather than themselves.[13] Additional studies report that even when people *think* about helping others, they activate a part of the brain called the mesolimbic pathway, which is responsible for feelings of gratification.[14] When humans serve others, the brain is doused with happiness chemicals such as dopamine, serotonin, oxytocin, and endorphins.[15] For example, our brains release dopamine when we love someone or something;[16] serotonin is activated when we feel appreciated, significant, or important,[17] and oxytocin is discharged by actions that convey emotional messages of kindness, caring, and love.[18] Endorphins are most easily released through exercise and laughter.[19]

Consider what it would take to inject all those euphoric chemicals at once. Setting aside your wants such as your time or your money requires love (dopamine release). It gives you a feeling of significance (serotonin release). It conveys a message of kindness and caring (oxytocin release), and it engenders a good response like laughter (endorphin release). As powerful as any drug, properly prioritizing and giving up wants infuses us with positive emotions and feelings of affirmation. While this doesn't always happen immediately, we usually feel positive emotions as we reflect back on our service or sacrifices.

Not only do these feel-good hormones help us physically, but they also affect our mental well-being in positive ways. An article in the *Chicago*

*Tribune,* "Be generous: It's a simple way to stay healthier," indicates that "The benefits of giving are significant.[20] The act of giving contributes to lower blood pressure, lower risk of dementia, less anxiety and depression, reduced cardiovascular risk, and overall greater happiness."[21]

**Where do positive feelings lead us?** Positive emotions amplify our ability to see and think clearly while increasing our creativity and problem-solving skills.[22] Let's examine the other half of "The Feeling Wheel" (shown below) that presents a list of positive emotions.[23] Both halves of the wheel are worth exploring to recognize the variety of emotions that affect us. Because positive emotions inspire us to act in helpful ways,[24] we can use them to identify and replace the negative emotions that could potentially take our brains hostage.[25] As you study the wheel, look for the emotions that seem the most familiar and comfortable to you.

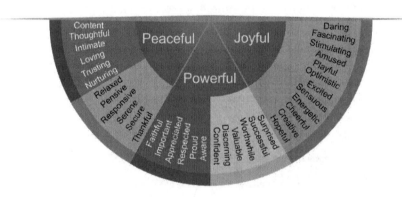

In our earlier discussion about the negative emotions segment, we discussed feeling offended. However, *not feeling offended* is legitimately missing from this half of the diagram. What is the antonym of *offended?* The opposite might be feeling confident. In the feeling wheel, *confident* is a subset of *powerful,* which is the opposite of the powerlessness that comes from being offended. Rarely do we take offense when we feel upright. Instead of allowing this negative emotion to consume us, sometimes we can use this hurt feeling as a tool to recognize a problem so we can reconcile a potential conflict or take control of a situation. By turning it around we act with confidence in ourselves and in an upright attitude—thus achieving greater success.

If the offense can't be turned into a positive feeling or outcome, at the very least we can recognize that the thing someone said or did was done unintentionally, in ignorance, or foolishly. Sometimes our right sidedness simply dictates that we allow the action to be the offender's responsibility and offer them empathy for their misstep. Because we can only take responsibility for what is in our control, we can choose to let go of the offensive action. By shedding the offense, we put ourselves in a more powerful position than if we allow it to hijack our emotions and give control to the offender.

For example, when content editors and peer reviewers disagreed with parts of this book, I could have been offended by their critical judgment. Instead, I chose the positive emotion of confidence (*their comments will make the book better*), success (*the book will be more successful if I consider their advice*), and gratitude (*I am thankful to have competent input*). I listened and made revisions accordingly.

Acceptance and thoughtful examination of criticism help us continue our journey with greater determination. We reach success more readily when we replace the negative emotions associated with opposition with positive emotions such as feeling optimistic, valuable, thankful, and secure.

**What is the bottom line?** We experience enduring happiness with others when we work together to get what we really want, choosing positivity and joy as the focus of our lives. Increased awareness of our emotions helps us mindfully tap into the connections between our wants, positive emotions, and their associated chemical responses. These happy hormones improve our physical and mental well-being. Working through opposition with positive emotions increases the likelihood of successfully overcoming conflict. Positive emotions promote rational solutions, strengthening our confidence, energy, and optimism.

## Connecting the Principles

Reflecting on your personal conflict experience, answer these questions:

- Can you identify any positive feelings you have experienced as you've attempted to solve your conflict?

- What types of service or sacrifice might improve the conflict or soften its impact?

- How might positive emotions help you better navigate this conflict and enable you to get what you really want?

## Segment 3. Rational Solutions

The rational solutions segment of the upright pyramid represents an open-minded, thoughtful approach to problem solving, suggesting we can evaluate a variety of pathways on which our wants may take us. *Rational* means agreeable to reason, having sound judgment, valid, and making good sense. Critical thinking is fundamental to rationality, and rationality requires intellectual honesty and a willingness to change as new information or evidence emerges.

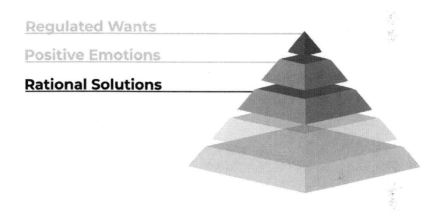

Regulated Wants

Positive Emotions

**Rational Solutions**

When we are rational, we carefully consider the Six Dimensions of Desire (chapter 3), including both patient or urgent wants, selfless or selfish desires, our level of discipline and commitment, the value of our wants, and moral or unethical ambitions. Rational thinking clears our heads and increases our capacity to consider alternative perspectives. Free from the fetters of a hijacked mind, we can be judicious, prudent, objective, and even thoughtful. The rational solutions segment describes emotional intelligence and the ability to create solutions for managing interpersonal relationships judiciously, logically, and empathetically.[26]

**What does it really mean to be rational?** The inherent complexity of wants requires us to evaluate and prioritize them continually. Open-mindedness, coupled with understanding, logic, and purpose, helps us confirm what we really want. Itemizing wants is one of the most distinguishing characteristics of a right-sided person. They can pick up wants like items at a yard sale, and in a moment, determine their genuine value or set them down, recognizing their worth or worthlessness. They behave rationally in the sense that they can discern the wants that will lead to what they really want.

A rational person may have a plan in their mind, but they are always open to other possibilities. Consider an executive team working together to approve the annual budget. As the year progresses and demands change, new, more rational solutions require the team to alter the budget, especially when an unexpected event, such as a pandemic, impacts their original plan.

Rational emotive behavior therapy hinges on the idea that absolutist or black-and-white thinking causes psychological discomfort and discord. Studies show that open-minded, flexible people live happier and more successful lives.[27] The Star Wars character Obi-Wan Kenobi affirms this principle when he rebukes his emotionally enraged apprentice, Anakin Skywalker, saying, "Only a Sith deals in absolutes!"[28] Moments later, poor upside-down Anakin is dismembered and tragically turns to the dark side.

Absolutes don't always work because they deny diverse human experiences and many other things we may not see or understand. Consideration tempers the rigidity of black-and-white thinking. Does this mean there is no truth? Of course not. What it does mean is that we, with our human emotion and imperfections, must learn to balance inevitable opposites with appropriate feelings and rational judgment.

As previously mentioned, positive emotions help us think clearly so we can form good judgment. With our reasonability intact, our intellectual response system can freely consider alternate possibilities. In the rational solutions segment of the pyramid, we see things that are generally invisible to an emotionally hijacked mind.

In contrast, have you ever witnessed an intense conversation between two people with differing points of view? An emotionally charged person may spout irrational statements that lack logical connections but are "certified as true" based on their volume and intensity. The opponent listens and then tries to insert a different perspective, only to get shut down with more emotional yet illogical allegations.

However, if both individuals remain rational, considerate, and dignified despite their diverse perspectives, they can logically and civilly agree to disagree without incident.

Consider Miguel, a reasonable and thoughtful person with consistent habits. Each day he takes the same route to work. On this day, as he passes through a familiar intersection, a car runs the stop sign, impacting the back end of his small-sized pickup truck. The crash rips the tailgate completely off the back of his truck. Miguel is okay. Of course, he didn't want the accident to happen, and even though it wasn't his fault, Miguel remains calm, looking for rational solutions and not allowing negative emotions to overcome him.

Even in this awful situation, Miguel accepts the fact that bad things happen. Still in his right mind, he rationally concludes that he needs to get out of his truck and assess the damage. He feels relieved he was not injured, and his thoughts then shift to concern for the other driver.

Miguel could have jumped out of his truck in an emotional fit and dramatically yelled, "Hey, are you drunk?!" or blurted, "You idiot! Were you texting your girlfriend?" or "Hey, [expletive]! Didn't you see the big red stop sign?"

What actually happened was that a lady in her mid-sixties on her way to the grocery store experienced a medical emergency and sailed through the intersection unconscious. Fortunately, Miguel remained rational because he sought to understand the situation before making assumptions, which enabled him to offer her medical assistance immediately.

False assumptions, a common form of irrationality, often lead to *misunderstanding* as we jump to conclusions without all the facts.[29] If we want to be a rational and thoughtful person, we must avoid false assumptions.

**What is the bottom line?** Rational solutions require logic, critical thinking, openness, and consideration. Avoiding absolutist thinking helps us stay flexible and balance the opposites we encounter in everyday life. When we choose positive emotions, we feel good, so critical thinking, problem solving, and rational creativity improve. Alternate options can be freely evaluated, accepted, or rejected while avoiding the pitfalls of absolutist thinking or false assumptions.

## Connecting the Principles

Using your personal conflict experience, consider personal insights you may have discovered from this segment:

- Is what you want rational or emotional?

- Have you considered other viewpoints?

- Have you verified all assumptions?

- Could there be a third alternative that may be even more reasonable?

## Segment 4. Proactive Actions

The *proactive* actions segment of the upright pyramid represents discipline in actively moving forward to solve a problem. While the *reactive* responses segment of the upside-down pyramid signified the unregulated responses we act out, this segment symbolizes the regulated physical manifestation of what we want. Even in the face of negative or challenging situations, an upright demeanor enables us to take proactive actions in anticipation of what we really want. A rationally thinking brain drives proactive actions, maintaining mental and physical control. Additionally, a proactive nature combines a forward-thinking focus with deliberate, thoughtful actions. With these two characteristics connected, we can overcome most conflicts.

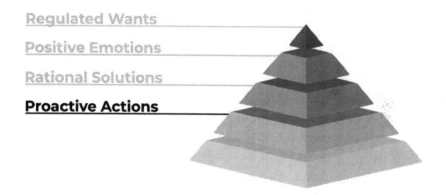

One of the greatest attributes of a proactive person is their capacity to do something that is hard but leads them to what they really want. They are willing to sacrifice some of their personal comfort or convenience because it is either the right thing to do, or it aligns with greater values and ethics. This is the essence of justness.

**What is justness, and how are proactive actions related?**
*Justness* means conformity to facts, truths, or rules. It is doing the right

things for the right reasons. Having a sense of justness allows us to change what *we* want to what someone else wants (assuming it's good), even if that alteration causes us some discomfort in the moment.

Justness places a higher value on the *harmony* of wants than it does on a singular want. Imagine yourself sitting in a baseball dugout. Your team is one game away from the playoffs. It's a tight contest, coming right down to the wire. In the bottom of the ninth inning, the score is tied 3-3. The manager turns momentarily from the intensity of the game and points his finger at you as you sit on the bench. "Step up, kid! Grab a bat and start warming up," he exclaims. Excitedly, you jump up, grab your equipment, and begin stretching.

A runner is toeing the bag at third base. There is one out. Your team needs to score a run to win the game and make the playoffs. As you step up to the plate, the manager gives you the sign to drop a sacrifice bunt along the first base line. The squeeze play would allow the runner on third base to come home, scoring the winning run. However, you realize that if you bunt, you will most likely be thrown out at first base, dropping your batting average from .299 to .298. (Your personal batting average doesn't matter to the manager.) That feels unfair! If you ignore the manager and swing away, you just might get a hit and increase your batting average to .300. Your personal goal of hitting .300 (which is outstanding by baseball standards) seems within your reach at this moment.[30] What do you do? You could let proactive actions settle the conflict; despite not *wanting* your personal batting average to go down, justness tells you it is the right thing to do—lay down a sacrifice bunt for the team to win the game.

We are emotional human beings with real wants. At first glance, we think we want things to be equal, fair, and just,[31] but sometimes we just want what *we* want, which may provoke upside-down tendencies.[32]

Richard Whately, an English rhetorician, put it this way: "A man is called selfish not for pursuing his own [wants], but for neglecting his neighbors."[33] The Proactive Actions segment of the upright pyramid helps us notice and overcome egocentric impulses—shifting us toward consideration for others and moving us closer to justness.

**How do we develop proactive actions?** Proactivity begins with our wants. As we control our wants using the Six Dimensions of Desire, positive emotions inherently free our minds from the fallacies of illogical conclusions. Boldly facing the challenges and oppositions of life gives us an opportunity to develop proactive problem-solving skills.

Stanford psychologist Carol Dweck describes this aspect of the upright pyramid with her concept of a growth mindset. She suggests we take charge, attack life with growth and improvement in mind, and purposefully choose to respond positively to opposition. These responses help fuel personal progress.[34]

Contrast this with what she describes as the fixed mindset, which coincides with the upside-down model and explains how we become victims of our own problems because we erroneously believe we have little or no control. Dweck's research documented astonishing results. She found that students who maintained a growth mindset experienced higher academic scores and greater success in their lives in contrast to those with fixed mindsets.[35]

We liberate ourselves from a fixed mindset through the process of proactively confronting negative conflicts with a positive approach. Consider the method of tempering metal, which entails heating the metal to a temperature just below the critical melting point, then allowing it to cool in still air. This procedure dramatically increases its overall strength. Working diligently through problems and difficulties similarly tempers us to become more resilient and capable individuals.

Likewise, we understand that strength and conditioning come through applied resistance. We don't usually go to the gym to sit and watch the morning news; we go there to proactively work with weight machines that provide resistance. The process of pressing against opposition strengthens us.

Studies show that experiencing adversity, like the tempering process or lifting weights, strengthens our psychological immune system. Trials build fortitude and resilience,[36] enabling us to deal with negative challenges more effectively.[37] Rather than becoming offended, angry, or helpless over injustice, a proactive person explores solutions and welcomes the growth that comes from trials and conflict. Herein lies the stark difference between choosing *proactive* actions over a *reactive* response.

Besides fortifying our strength, proactivity helps stimulate open-mindedness.[38] We are not just looking for the silver lining, but for gold, bronze, or platinum linings too. Studies indicate that this habit of open-mindedness helps increase happiness.[39] Buddha reaffirmed this by saying, "Let yourself be open, and life will be easier." Open-mindedness is the catalyst to optimism, which leads to happiness; closed-minded thinking is mired in pessimism.

The base of the upright pyramid becomes wider and increasingly stable with proactive actions like consideration and openness. We employ the concept of justness through familiar tenets such as turning the other cheek, going the extra mile, doing good to those who hate us, and giving more than is asked. We proactively serve others with consideration by cleaning up, giving to the poor, lending a helping hand, and loving those who are difficult to love. If we truly want to behave in upright ways, we do all this without resentment or expecting favors in return. Developing these proactive skills requires self-awareness, patience, and the practice of all the previous principles in the upright pyramid.

**How do we best respond when things go wrong?** Everything eventually falls apart! The second law of thermodynamics, also known as entropy, affects every aspect of life on Earth. The universe constantly moves from a state of order to a state of disorder. That brand new car on the showroom floor with every component in perfect order will fall apart eventually. This same law applies to our physical bodies. No one escapes this world alive. When we understand this law of inevitability, we are more likely to face obstacles, trials, failures, disappointments, personal insults, and unmet expectations with patience and proactivity.

Lou Gehrig perfectly exemplifies proactive action as he faced a tragic illness. Nicknamed the "Iron Horse," he was a gifted athlete who played first base for the New York Yankees from 1923 to 1939. In the prime of his baseball career, at the age of 36, Gehrig was struck by amyotrophic lateral sclerosis (ALS), a progressive, neurodegenerative disease. Knowing the magnitude of his illness and where his life was headed, he stood before a large crowd of fans at Yankee Stadium and gave a right-sided farewell address. After listing the blessings of his life—his parents, his wife, his teammates, and the many good games in which he had played—he said, "Today, I consider myself the luckiest man on the face of the earth.... I might have been given a bad break, but I've got an awful lot to live for."

Two years later and shortly before he died, he called a friend to share news about a recent breakthrough that doctors had made in treating what came to be known as "Lou Gehrig's Disease." He explained that nine out of ten patients given a particular medicine had improved. His friend immediately asked him if he was one of the nine. Gehrig replied, "Well, it didn't work on me. But how about that for an average? Nine out of ten! Isn't that great?"

Lou Gehrig *didn't want* ALS. But despite his suffering and a career cut short, he maintained an upright attitude all the way to the end.

We all experience losses, such as unexpected illness, the death of a loved one, the breakup of a relationship, termination from a job, or bankruptcy. But if we handle our disappointments with proactive actions, we can remain more objective and work through them with resilience.[40] When we acknowledge difficulty and accept obstacles with grace, we can proactively make the necessary corrections to bring what we want *most* back into alignment.

---

> Rather than becoming offended, angry, or helpless, a proactive person explores the growth that comes from trials and conflict.

---

The airline industry illustrates this pattern. Every departing flight has a destination, but along the way, the aircraft is constantly being blown off course by wind, weather, and navigational errors. Instead of disappointment or frustration, the pilot takes proactive measures, making small course corrections that lead the aircraft to its intended destination.

Sometimes we create our own conflict, and when we do so, we must hold ourselves accountable for our *own* actions. Likewise, the quicker we correct directional errors and make necessary adjustments, the more likely we are to get what we *really* want at the end of our journey.

### How do we stay proactive in the face of intentional harm?

Conflict can occur because another person intentionally harms us. Proactive people resist becoming victims by remaining positive and in control even during distress. Positive emotions, rational solutions, and proactive actions help us navigate intentional wrongdoing.

Thoughtful regard for others also can heal wounds that otherwise appear incurable. "Seeking first to understand," as the late Stephen R. Covey suggested, shows both empathy and consideration.[41] It means we stop to think about alternate perspectives, expanding our understanding and enabling us to feel what others feel before we form conclusions.

Similarly, the proactive actions segment incorporates forgiveness, a gracious form of empathy. The word *forgive* has an interesting etymology.

*For* is a prefix meaning "away." *Give* means to present voluntarily and without expecting compensation. Together, *for-give* means to give away without expecting compensation. Making the conscious decision to pardon another for their faults (including ourselves) while leaving resentment behind allows us to be empathetic and merciful. Being forgiving is one of the most noble virtues of a proactive person.

Forgiving ourselves is just as important as forgiving others. What would it take to let go of negative emotions and the untrue messages that we might be telling ourselves? Proactive actions help us rise above pessimism, allowing us to do what we really want to do and become who we really want to be.

Psychologist Michael McCullough reinforces the proactive nature required for thoughtful forgiveness. He explains "You have to have some way of maintaining relationships, even though it's inevitable some will harm your interests, given enough time. The forgiveness instinct enables people to suppress the desire for revenge and signal their willingness to continue, even though someone has harmed their interests, assuming the person will refrain from doing so again in the future."[42]

Victoria Ruvolo's story exemplifies both proactive principles of forgiveness and suppressing the desire for revenge. She was driving home in November 2004 when a high school student dropped a 20-pound frozen turkey from an overpass that smashed through her windshield, bending the steering wheel before striking her in the head and nearly killing her. Doctors had to wire her jaw shut and surgically rebuild her face. Victoria, who was 44 at the time, spent nearly a month in the hospital recovering from this tragedy. The young man who threw the turkey was arrested and charged with first-degree assault, reckless endangerment, forgery, criminal mischief, and criminal possession of stolen property. He faced up to 25 years in prison, but Victoria lobbied the district attorney to give the teen a plea deal that only required him to serve six months in jail. While Victoria could have passively watched justice take its course, she remarkably chose to improve the situation for herself and the young man.

"Instead of making a snap decision, I wanted to know more," Victoria said. "I started asking questions. I wanted to know about this kid."

After his tearful guilty plea, Victoria hugged the young man in court and urged him, "Do good with your life."

"I took him from being this terrible ogre and made him human. That's what we all need to do. Just take a step back," Victoria said.

---

Being forgiving is one of the most noble
virtues of a proactive person.

---

Her proactive compassion and thoughtful choice to forgive this young person freed him from a life of misery. What's more, Victoria released herself from the fetters of hatred, which could have sentenced her to a life of bitterness.

Victoria took a proactive approach and dedicated the rest of her life to speak about the power of forgiveness, providing yet another example of what a proactive person with an upright perspective looks like.

It may feel difficult, but it is not impossible!

**What is the bottom line?** Proactive action, the fourth segment of the upright pyramid, represents *action* versus *reaction* to both internal and external forces. This segment employs justness, suggesting we do things for the right reasons. We remain upright by sacrificing impatient, egocentric, undisciplined wants for more beneficial, treasured, and worthwhile wants. A proactive approach prompts us to remain positive even under difficult circumstances, encouraging us to change when we are wrong and to forgive others who have wronged us.

Proactive actions produce opportunities for resolving conflict. This opens the door to the remarkable last segment of the upright pyramid—the powerful position.

## Connecting the Principles

Consider what proactive actions you can apply to your personal conflict experience:

- How could justness change your approach to the conflict?

- What proactive approach could help resolve this conflict?

## Segment 5. Powerful Position

The final segment of the upright pyramid symbolizes the powerful position. Together, all the attitudes and behaviors represented in the previous segments produce stable, strong attributes. These characteristics and choices culminate in placing a person in a more powerful position by enhancing their respect and trustworthiness. Respectful relationships form the basis of personal power. Without positive relationships, we feel powerless and alone.

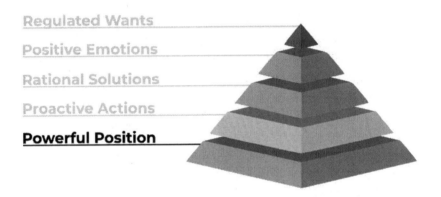

Regulated Wants

Positive Emotions

Rational Solutions

Proactive Actions

**Powerful Position**

When we harmonize our wants, positive feelings and camaraderie expand to create a feeling of teamwork. Cooperation enhances productivity and draws in other people who want to be part of something bigger. Sharing an open-minded approach to problem solving contributes to an upright culture within companies, families, and communities. This upright culture expands the powerful position because it elevates individuals, fosters encouragement, and engages communication, creativity, and innovation.[43]

Championship sports teams validate the essence of the powerful position. Year after year we watch champions honor, thank, and praise each other for their extraordinary teamwork throughout a challenging season. Even the burliest football players talk about how much they love their teammates and coaches. These positive emotions of unity and admiration are not just found on the sports field but also prevail in the best businesses and within close personal relationships.

**What does a powerful leader look like?** The upright pyramid illustrates attributes[44] of true leadership.[45] Rather than pushing people from behind to get what they want, genuine leaders inspire their teams by example as they work faithfully alongside them. A natural affection attracts friends and coworkers to join in the pursuit of success.

The influence of an upright leader increases naturally over time and cannot be demanded.[46] When we truly possess the power of influence, we don't need to recite our best qualities or publicize our integrity.[47]

Martin Luther King Jr.'s passionate dream for justice and equality inspired all humanity. Florence Nightingale, nicknamed the Lady with the Lamp, worked tirelessly alongside her nurses, making nightly rounds to tend the sick and injured. George Washington inspired his men during the battle of Princeton as he boldly rode his horse back and forth along the front lines of the combat. What the world needs desperately right now are upright people who demonstrate this type of inspirational leadership!

Our base of influence expands when we care about others and strive to promote their best qualities. We can be builders rather than destroyers! This abundance mentality and selfless approach leads to respectful and emotionally connected relationships.[48] Cooperative success flourishes when we want the people around us to succeed.[49]

# Harmony and Honor

The roundabout intersection analogy described in chapter 2 illustrates the foundational principle of harmony and how it connects with our wants. Observing the rules of the road in a harmonized way allows each driver the opportunity to interact then proceed to their intended destination. This brief interplay also requires respect for the other drivers. Harmony and respect go hand in hand to promote peace, regard, and consideration.

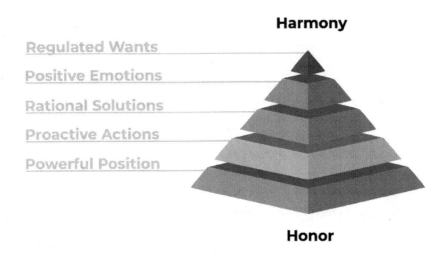

**Harmony**

Regulated Wants

Positive Emotions

Rational Solutions

Proactive Actions

Powerful Position

**Honor**

Likewise, citizens in a harmonious community relinquish selfish, unregulated wants for the civility, fairness, and safety of their community. In both situations, harmony of wants produces an atmosphere of honor.

## How Loyalty Builds Harmony

We cultivate successful relationships in the home, at work, and in the community by rooting them in loyalty. For example, because I love you, my willingness to consider what you want multiplies—assuming those wants are reasonable. When we genuinely and unselfishly seek the welfare of others, trust and honor naturally elevate both of us.[50]

A Greek legend told by Cicero describes a man named Pythias and his friend Damon. As they traveled to Syracuse during the reign of the tyrannical Dionysius I, Pythias spoke evil of the king. He was subsequently arrested for his outspoken resistance and sentenced to death for plotting against the king.

Before his execution, Pythias pleaded to be allowed to return home one last time to settle his affairs and bid his family farewell. Not wanting to be taken for a fool, the king refused, believing that if Pythias was released, he would flee and never return. Surprisingly, Pythias' friend Damon offered himself as a hostage in Pythias' absence. The king was intrigued by this proposition and insisted that if Pythias did not return by the appointed time, Damon would be executed in his stead. Damon resolutely agreed to these conditions, and Pythias was released.

The day Pythias promised to return came and went. King Dionysius scoffed at the situation and called for Damon's execution—but just as the executioner prepared to kill Damon, Pythias stumbled onto the scene!

Apologizing to his friend for the delay, Pythias explained that on the passage back to Syracuse, pirates had captured his ship and thrown him overboard. With all the effort he could muster, he swam to shore and made his way back to Syracuse as quickly as possible, arriving just in time to save his friend. King Dionysius was so astonished and charmed by their harmonious and loyal friendship that he pardoned both men.[51]

## How Reliability Leads to Honor

Confidence increases with consistency. Each time we tell the truth and follow through with what we promise, we build trust and respect in our reliability. To become truly honorable, we must tell the truth and keep the promises we make. Saying no to those things you cannot commit to—so you can honor what you already have promised—is just as important as saying yes and following through. We must fulfill our verbal commitments, live up to agreements in contracts, and be responsible if we want respect.

Increasing reliability improves predictability. People tend to admire and trust those who prove to be dependable. We can predict a future pattern or behavior when things appear in order. For example, the next letter in this sequence is easy to predict:

J, K, L, M, N, O ...

The next letter is obviously P. We are confident in our knowledge and understanding of the future when things are set in order. In contrast, chaos equals randomness. The next letter in this sequence is impossible to guess:

J, F, T, P, J, B ...

This sequence is unpredictable because the letters are "out of order." We tend to avoid things that are erratic and uncertain. Who in their right mind would get on an elevator when there is a handwritten note that says, "out of order"? Who wants to associate with a person who behaves unpredictably? Like most lucrative financial investments, respect and value must be earned over time. We can't go to the dollar store and pick up a cheap pack of respect. We can't borrow it, and we had better not demand it. Demanding honor or respect by virtue of, age, gender, position, race, or any other self-serving aspiration entirely depreciates it.

---

Respectful relationships form the basis of personal power.

---

The unpredictable boss with shifting demands loses honor with employees over time. Respect can only be won through harmony and mutual consideration. We can't force respect. It bestows itself naturally upon those who are predictable and upright. The late Prime Minister Margaret Thatcher put it this way: "Being powerful is like being a lady. If you have to tell people you are, you aren't."

# The Result of Regulated Wants

*Regulated wants* produce *positive emotions* that promote *rational solutions*. In addition, regulated wants inspire *proactive actions*, even amid adversity. Together, these attributes put us in a *powerful position* where we develop a more positive influence on the people and relationships around us. Consistency and dependability endow us over time with respect, honor, admiration, and appreciation. As we increase our influence for good and elevate others, we also enhance our ability to choose what we *really* want.

Strength and stability naturally define an upright person. However, none of us are as strong and stable as we would like to be. Alexander Pope correctly penned, "To err is human." Any chance of staying right sided takes recognition, awareness, effort, and a periodic self-evaluation. We should maintain awareness of what we really want by making daily course corrections and pursuing paths that lead to additional investments in harmony and honor.

When our wants are ordered, harmonious, and predictable to others, we begin metaphorically to build an upright pyramid effect, which then helps us become *respectable* and *powerful!* As we align ourselves and our desires (top of the pyramid) with consideration for others and ethical standards of conduct, the results naturally culminate in a wide base of power (bottom of the pyramid). This defines regulated wants that are well founded on what we really want. These are the wants that are properly calculated, sufficiently thought out, and lead a person to a flourishing future.

The two metaphorical pyramids presented thus far illustrate a strikingly different series of causes and effects that each begin with *want*. The following two statements summarize what we have learned:

- **The problem:** Unregulated, disharmonic wants can cause us to feel upside down, unsettled, and powerless—leading to disharmony and dishonor with other people or entities.

- **The solution:** Regulated, harmonic wants lead to feeling upright, stable, and strong—improving harmony and honor with other people and entities.

The graphic below illustrates the problem and the solution.

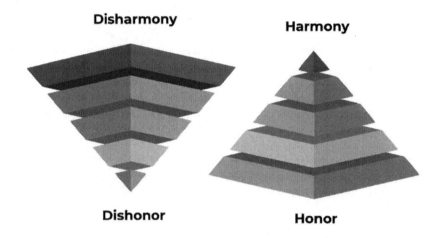

With this valuable insight, how are you going to solve the personal conflict experience you recorded at the beginning of this book?

You know the problem. You also know the solution. But how do you make the mental transformation?

In the next section, two specific tools describe how to turn upside-down responses to our wants into more powerful, upright action!

The first tool, *The Core*, provides a methodology for flipping over almost any upside-down situation or attitude using four specific expressions.

The second tool, *The Consensus Diagram*, details a three-part plan to help root out the most common causes of conflict. This tool reveals the underlying assumptions within our wants and provides a technique for resolving them.

Together, these tools assist in constructing a stable, upright character that engenders our true values, considers the needs of others, and builds our self-mastery.

# THE APPLICATION

*The conversion from behaving in upside-down ways to developing upright habits requires more than awareness. This section presents two methodologies to help you create a more stable, sustainable, connected life that aligns with your highest values.*

# CHAPTER 7

# CHANGING DIRECTION

*"Consideration is the soil in which wisdom may be expected to grow."*

—Ralph Waldo Emerson

One beautiful morning, I was happily on my way to a construction site to see how the excavation work was coming along. As I drove, my phone rang. It was the backhoe operator I was going to visit.

"I have really bad news!" he said abruptly in a frustrated tone.

"What's the problem?"

"I just hit a major underground phone cable. There are a thousand strands of colored wire poking out of the ditch!" he exclaimed.

A weight dropped to the bottom of my stomach. "Didn't we call for locates? That area was cleared for digging, right?" I asked in hesitation.

"Yes, it was cleared, there were no markings in this area," the worker declared. "But we have a serious problem on our hands! What are you going to do about it?"

I was keenly aware of the problem. A thousand strands of broken wire needed to be fixed, but I didn't have the slightest idea about how to put them back together. I needed someone with skills, tools, and expertise to help me.

That's exactly where we are in this book. Instead of having a mess of wires poking out of the ground, we have identified a mess of conflicted or unregulated wants disrupting our lives. We must convert uncertainty into something more secure and predictable. We know that an upside-down response to our wants creates a problem. We also know that reacting with an upright approach solves most problems. But how are we going to make that change happen? What will it take to fix the problem?

## The Core: A Tool for Regulating Wants

Between the two pyramids sits the control mechanism: the device or tool providing the means to overcome conflict and increase empowerment. I call this instrument for success *The Core* (illustrated by the circle between the two pyramids).

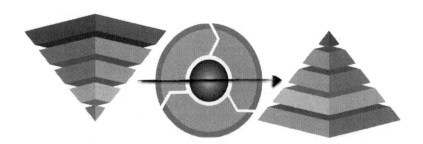

The Core functions like a processing plant positioned between the two opposing models. Four powerful principles embedded within The Core help facilitate the transformation from upside down to right side up.

Think of the core like the gym we talked about earlier, where we lift weights to become fit, healthy, and strong. We don't go there to hang out or watch others exercise; we go there to work, sweat, and push ourselves to new limits. Working through The Core is much the same. It encourages us to sculpt our wants, tone our emotions, and build our reasonability skills. Most importantly, in The Core we specifically address the Six Dimensions of Desire, practice harmony with others, and shed undesirable conflict.

Because The Core acts as a processing center, we might enter its doors feeling pessimistic, emotional, conflicted, or unsettled. As we work through the four principles, judiciously practicing each of the precepts, we can walk out feeling energized, happy, empowered, and upright!

Think of The Core as having a personal membership to a gym with access to equipment available for your use. It's *your* Core. You make an investment in it, then go there as often as you can—or neglect going there. It takes a commitment that comes from deep within you and originates from what you *really want*. You can't fake The Core or pretend to apply its principles and still get results, nor should you saunter through it half-heartedly. True, deep-rooted change comes through earnest effort.

There may be times when you fail to live up to the high standards or principles found within The Core. That is not a failure—try again. Once you master the principles, you can more fully embrace them, allowing them to take deeper root within you.

# Four Conventions of The Core

Imagine a gym with four distinct pieces of equipment. All four are necessary to achieve balance and maximum fitness. Just as you wouldn't use a squat rack to strengthen every part of your body, you should not rely on any *single* convention of The Core to fix an upside-down situation. Other than the central principle of consideration, the three other conventions operate in no specific order. They are interconnected, working together like the various strength and cardio machines in a gym to produce comprehensive results. Some conflicts or limitations prompt us to start with one piece of equipment, while other circumstances suggest that we wisely begin with another. *It is imperative to understand that we must carefully choose to start with the right approach.* Just like following a carefully devised fitness plan, we won't necessarily use all of The Core conventions every time, or use them in the same order, because every situation requires a different application.

## Begin with Consideration

The fundamental and uncompromising principle underlying all the conventions of The Core is *Begin with Consideration*. We might relate this to what Stephen R. Covey called the fifth habit: "Seek first to understand before being understood." Covey taught, "Most people do not listen with the intent to understand; they listen with the intent to reply."[1] *Begin with Consideration* implies we offer empathy and attention *before* seizing them. It means we use kindness in how we treat each other, even in the face of opposition.

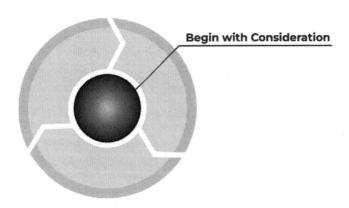

**Begin with Consideration**

**What is true consideration?** The word *consider* comes from the Latin *considerare*, meaning to look at closely, observe, or to examine. When a doctor examines a patient, she inspects and scrutinizes the problem carefully. The symptoms could be the result of disease A, disease B, or a disease previously unknown to her. Occasionally, a doctor may fail to consider all the symptoms and make a false diagnosis.

The suffix *-tion* in the word *consideration* expresses an action or a state of being. Therefore, *consideration* is the act of considering or the act of examining. A person with consideration can examine a subject one way, then turn it over and view it from a completely different perspective. Negative emotions do not ruin their reasoning abilities.

*Begin with Consideration* means enlarging our minds to imagine other possibilities. Consideration is about being curious while also being courteous. A considerate person is polite and genuinely concerned about the thoughts and feeling of others. Consideration denotes our ability *to pause, listen, think carefully about,* and *contemplate* another person's wants, challenging us to take a fresh view of ourselves and the world around us. With a high degree of consideration, personal beliefs become subordinate to actual truth. Consideration is being teachable, receptive, and open to new ideas.

Let's analyze a real conversation to explore how consideration plays out and how its role affects our progress and perspective.

"Hey, Jacob," Bryanna politely announced as she stepped gingerly into his office.

"Hello, Bry," he responded pleasantly, looking up from his work. "What's up?"

"I just got off the phone with one of our former clients who told me something very interesting."

"What's that?" Jacob inquired.

"She said she stopped using our Debut 42 last year because she couldn't figure out how to make it work properly."

Jacob sighed, "She obviously didn't watch the instruction video."

"Actually," Bryanna affirmed, "she watched it several times, but it didn't make sense to her. The reason she called me today was to tell me that she watched another person use the Debut 42, and then it totally made sense to her! Now that she gets it, she wants to start ordering again."

"Wait, what made the difference?" Jacob asked.

"She said it was how the instruction video was made. It was shot from an observer's point of view, but in real life, she saw how it worked from the user's perspective. That new frame of reference made all the difference in her understanding."

"Well, she must not have watched the video closely enough," Jacob refuted. "We put a lot of time and research into that video."

"Yes, but the perspective in the video is wrong," Bry countered.

"Well, there is no way we are going to reshoot that video!"

"Jacob, if we reshoot it, maybe sales will increase because more people will understand how to use the Debut 42. You know how complicated that product can be."

"It is not that complicated. Besides, we don't have the time or the budget to reshoot the video," Jacob said as he waived the back of his hand at Bry, dismissing her from his office.

If we step back from this story, we might imagine how Bryanna might have felt about her boss at the end of that conversation. Perhaps she was feeling a bit upside down by Jacob's refusal to consider the customer's feedback. He simply did not *want* any input.

The inability to consider another person's perspective significantly hinders improvement projects. Skeptical rebuttals such as, "It will cost too much money," or, "We don't have the time," could be understood as, "I don't want to spend money," and/or, "I don't want to do it again." A lack of consideration prevents us from innovating solutions or thinking outside our box.

The following story further illustrates this principle and how consideration either impedes or enhances our vision. A respected senior friend called me one day and asked if I could come over to help her print some photos. The Windows 98 print software with which she was so familiar was not installed on the new laptop she had just purchased. I went right over to help my dear friend, who I'll call Molly. The first thing Molly said was, "I *want* my old photo software reinstalled."

"Okay," I said as I sat down at her computer. "Actually, everything you need is built into your new system. Watch what I do and then give it a try."

"I just want my old photo printing software back," she murmured.

"Molly, it's really not that difficult—just watch what I do," I coaxed.

She continued talking, not listening to or looking at what I was trying to show her. "This will never work like I want it to. I just want you to install that old software and bring back all my photos and...."

As she continued her rant, I got up from the desk, walked to the window and stood silently, looking out at the landscape, waiting for her to conclude her tirade.

"What?" she asked incredulously after my stillness began to bother her.

"Molly, I can see this change is difficult for you and you're struggling with learning a new way to print your photos. That said, your old software will not install onto your new computer. They don't work together. Let me ask you this question: what do you *really* want? Do you want the *software*, or do you want to be able to *print* your photos? If you want to print your photos, then can you please consider watching what I am about to show you?"

After considering, then recognizing what she really wanted, Molly turned her attention to this free and easier way of printing and managing the photos on her computer. A little empathy from me and consideration on her part allowed her to get what she really wanted.

**How are empathy and consideration related?** Empathy is a form of consideration. Psychologist Sterling G. Ellsworth defines empathy as a "... deep respect for human feeling; it is the ability to listen, understand, and be sensitive—to *feel* the feelings of others and communicate [our understanding] back to them."[2] Showing empathy diffuses confrontations with emotionally hijacked people while also honoring their feelings and reinforcing our acceptance of them.

We best communicate empathy for others when we listen without injecting judgment. Ellsworth further explains that empathizing does not include giving advice, agreeing, or disagreeing; rather, it is "following the other person's lead to discover how he or she feels.... A person in this position needs emotional first aid: someone to understand first and simply accept what is going on inside him, someone to give empathy. Then after he feels loved, accepted, and understood, he will have more strength to deal with the problems." Ellsworth's description perfectly exemplifies The Core principle of *Begin with Consideration*.

---

Consideration means we offer empathy
and attention before seizing them.

---

Besides offering empathy to others, we can empathize with and forgive ourselves. *Begin with Consideration* helps us acknowledge the realities of negative emotions that hijack reasoning skills. Then we can choose to reverse those emotions, replace them with positive feelings, and reopen our minds to new possibilities. Studies suggest that applying self-consideration can help us overcome negative events more than self-confidence can.[3]

**What is the difference between "I want" and "I'm looking for..."?** My friend Matteo called me one day in January. With convincing words, he said, "Scott, you want to go skiing with me today! There is so much fresh powder—you want to take advantage of that!" Notwithstanding his excellent persuasion and selling techniques, I replied with certitude, "I wish I could, Matteo, but what I am looking for is the time to finish my book. If I buckle down today and get it done, we could go next week. In fact, we could go a few times next week."

"I want ..." usually focuses on one paralyzing preference, often coupled with strong emotions. If we feel upside down because we can't have exactly what we want, we might take nothing at all. Remember the example of family members who argued over the specific terms of a will? We can become so focused on what we want (money or items) that we end up with less than we originally desired. Just like the example above, sometimes our wants can be intensely focused. "I want to go skiing today," leaves little room for other choices. The phrase *I want* has laser-point passion built into it, disallowing diversity, variation, or alternatives.

To *look for* significantly differs from *I want* because it is a transitional statement rather than a definitive declaration. It indicates openness and consideration while demonstrating a humble search for solutions. *I'm looking for* reveals a spirit of curiosity that can lead to creative problem solving and more plentiful opportunities.[4] In the illustration below, notice how the upside-down demand *I want!* is fixated on one paralyzing point: the circle.

By focusing on only one object, we miss any other perspectives that may possibly be better choices. By contrast, I'm *looking for* … considers a variety of options and keeps us open to finding a solution that we may not already visualize. A suitable choice could be the circle, the square, or possibly some other shape.

If we don't get what we explicitly want, lost expectations can trigger negative emotions that may cause us to feel upside down. However, when we say, "I am looking for …" we tend to stay positive, recognizing potential solutions more readily.

Consider this situation. Roger stops by the grocery store on his way home from work to pick up a few items for the dinner party he and his wife are hosting tonight. After scurrying through the store with a basket full of goodies, Roger confronts three long lines at the registers. That is not what he *wants*. What he is *looking for* is the fastest way out of the store, but the line he has currently selected has come to a screeching halt.

An elderly woman, fumbling through her purse in search of her checkbook, creates a bottleneck. Behind her, a twenty-something, rough-looking dude is making a ruckus with insulting statements toward the poor old woman. Even the checkout clerk expresses her exasperation with the geriatric obstruction.

"Hey lady, just use a card," the dude snarls.

Checking his watch, Roger scans the other two lines to see if they are moving any faster. Deadlocked, Roger looks for an alternative to get the line moving.

"We ain't got all night!" the rude ruffian announces.

Considering his options, Roger notices her total charge is only eleven dollars. He pulls out his wallet, steps past the mean man, and taps his credit card on the reader for the woman. Embarrassed, she begins to protest.

"Ma'am, it's my pleasure," Roger assures with a smile.

The young man stares at him in disbelief.

How does this story apply to the principles so far? The upright, proactive approach Roger took of looking for positive outcomes helped him discover a rational solution to an otherwise frustrating problem. This form of consideration helps us use creative means to fulfill our ultimate desires.

It is important to remember that upright people assert themselves graciously and are not pushovers. They know what they *really* want and are determined to get it, but not in an impatient, inconsiderate, right-here, right-now kind of way.

If we can learn to exchange the demanding *I want!* for the more flexible *I'm looking for,* we develop upright characteristics as we work methodically toward our goals. Our composure increases with our confident, self-disciplined approach. We become more patient as we expand our capacity to endure delays and are better able to face adversity calmly and with hopeful optimism. Studies show we reduce conflict and increase cooperation[5] as we practice patience.[6]

I invite you to try using *I'm looking for* today and see what happens.

**How can resistance become a valuable opportunity to learn?** It is important to remember that a lack of consideration demonstrates resistance to change. In the April 2009 *Harvard Business Review* article entitled, "Decoding Resistance to Change," Jeffrey and Laurie Ford explain, "It's true that resistance can be irrational and self-serving. But like it or not, it is an important form of feedback. Dismissing it robs you of a powerful tool as you implement change. If you can gain perspective by paying attention to, understanding, and learning from behaviors you perceive as threatening, you will ultimately deliver better results."[7]

The Fords masterfully explain how leaders (or anyone who wants to practice upright skills) can learn from resistance. "Blaming resisters is not only pointless but can actually lead to destructive managerial behaviors.

When managers perceive resistance as a threat, they may become competitive, defensive, or uncommunicative. They are sometimes so concerned with being right—and not looking bad—that they lose sight of their original goals. In stubbornly pushing things through without understanding the resistance, they sacrifice goodwill, put valuable relationships in jeopardy, and squander the opportunity to engage skeptics in service of a better plan. They don't hear about missing pieces and faulty assumptions. And, in true us-versus-them fashion, they presume that only the other folks—the resisters—need to alter their behavior, and that the change would succeed if not for the resisters' irrational and self-serving actions."[8]

When approached thoughtfully to explore and understand its origins, resistance can be used as a resource for overcoming conflict instead of creating it, and *Begin with Consideration* encourages us to leverage opposition in beneficial ways. Typically, resistance to new things indicates one of two scenarios: either fear of uncertainty and change, or an unintended consequence that hasn't been fully considered but which the antagonist sees. Behind every resistant response lies some emotional or personal experience that roused it into existence. By drawing upon the experience of another person, we may discover hidden insights.

> ## Consideration is about being curious
> ## while also being courteous.

How can we address those concerns to uncover more information before moving on? Instead of starting a volleyball game of "yeah, but…," we can stop the conflict by applying empathy as we "seek first to understand." This mutual act of trust helps both sides of the conflict better expand each other's knowledge and perspective—while dispelling skepticism.

When we use consideration to embrace resistance (and its underlying concerns) with compassion, we break the barriers of conflict through our empathetic response and willingness to explore the problem. A small dose of consideration can greatly improve unity and respect, especially when the other person perceives that you care about what they want, how they feel, and what they know.[9] Once the concerns are understood for both sides, then the reasons for each perspective can be thoughtfully factored into new, more innovative solutions.

**What is the bottom line?** The Core is the tool for turning an upside-down pyramid over. *Begin with Consideration* sits firmly at the center of The Core. The principle of consideration means enlarging our minds to imagine other possibilities and being kind, courteous, polite, and empathetic, especially in situations of resistance or conflict. With thoughtful intent, we can express interest in and explore the ideas and feeling of others.

---

Consideration displays a disciplined
and optimistic approach.

---

When we apply consideration, we analyze conflict with openness, seeking broader perspectives from others' emotional and logical insights. Instead of using the more closed-minded "I want," we can use the more open phrase, "I'm looking for...." This type of response reduces conflict because we are open to other's wants.

Consideration helps to discover and overcome underlying problems that cause resistance to change, which opens the door to innovative solutions and successful outcomes. *Begin with Consideration* forms the foundation upon which the other elements of The Core rest. It supports the remaining conventions and provides rich soil in which they can grow.

## Connecting the Principles

Reviewing your personal conflict experience, think about the following:

- How can you apply consideration and empathy to your conflict?

- How might the phrase "I'm looking for ..." help you increase your consideration and openness?

- If you are encountering resistance, how can you explore opposition to discover new ideas or dispel skepticism?

## Just Say Okay

Once consideration is in full swing, we can continue the process of regulating conflicted wants. How could we suspend a problem to create the time and space to analyze it, to consider more perspectives, to contemplate various solutions? We can just say "okay."

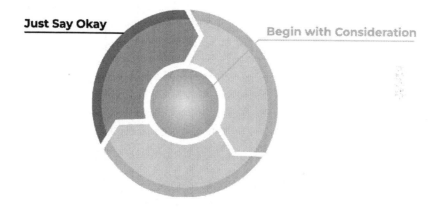

Commonly used in the English language, *okay* means "proceeding normally; satisfactory or under control."[10] We use the word all the time without even thinking about it. It merely communicates that "I agree to *hear* you even though I don't necessarily agree with you." This form of *okay* simply continues the dialogue with consideration. When judiciously employed between people who share mutual trust and respect, this classic utterance can swiftly disarm rising conflict and regulate an emotional situation.

Let me emphasize one vital point: you will never know the power of *Just Say Okay* until you actually use it. The genesis of *Just Say Okay* came from Michael. Because saying *yes* to my suggestion of moving him to Delancy Street was too much of a commitment and emotionally difficult for him, saying *okay* allowed Michael the chance to pause long enough to consider what he really wanted. *Just Say Okay* was the step he needed to gather his wits until he could think rationally through the options and make the best choice.

**A word of warning!** DO NOT *JUST SAY OKAY* IN CIRCUMSTANCES OF DANGER, ABUSE, BULLYING, MANIPULATION, DISREGARD FOR LAW, PERSONAL SAFETY, OR ANY SITUATION THAT COULD COMPROMISE A PERSON'S WELL-BEING.

*Just Say Okay* should specifically be used to defuse conflict kindly with those you trust. It should only be invoked when it diminishes danger, not when it amplifies risk.

Jordan Peterson wisely warns, "I am morally obliged to bargain as hard on my own behalf as they are on theirs. If I fail to do so, I will end up a slave and the other person a tyrant."[11]

If a potentially perilous or manipulative situation threatens you, the other two conventions of The Core (introduced later in this chapter) should be employed instead of *Just Say Okay*.

**Are we agreeing with an opponent when we say *okay*?** *Just Say Okay* is not an agreement with something we oppose; it is not the same as saying *yes* definitively. When used correctly, it simply communicates that we have chosen to take another person's ideas into consideration.[12] An utterance of *okay* is merely a polite acknowledgement without a full commitment. This is an agreement to *consider* where we stand with the purposes of exploring the rationale, preventing further conflict, and removing the emotion from the situation.

Saying *okay* flows naturally and simply communicates, "I hear what you are saying, so let's both pause together to recognize all the angles before we move on." In the face of conflict, saying *okay* can actively stop an intensifying situation; it disengages the battle, allowing us to move forward civilly with thoughtful self-control. Think of it as an informal time out—a momentary pause allowing us to take a step back, inhale a deep breath, and clear our heads to look at the bigger picture. It also provides a means of taking a closer look at a situation before doing anything with it. Like a yield sign at an intersection, *Just Say Okay* means to pause then analyze the situation before proceeding to our intended destination.

> We must be judicious about when to say
> *okay* because some situations require that
> we use a different convention of The Core.

Once hopeful optimism and trust have been established, it becomes easier to explore the true wants behind the conflict. It communicates that we are willing to be vulnerable together as we evaluate the arguments. *Just Say Okay* can be a good way to "agree with thine adversary quickly, whiles thou art in the way with him."[13] This doesn't necessarily mean you will go along with everything your adversary suggests, but that you will consider what your adversary is saying in order to keep the negotiation alive. This sincere form of respect engenders empathy and helps build a relationship of trust in conflicting circumstances.[14]

The following example shows how this may play out in a common family conflict.

"I want a dog," my teenage son boldly announced to my wife (who dislikes dogs).

"Okay…," my wife responded with some trepidation, trying to stay calm.

"Wait, what did you say?" my son stammered in disbelief.

"I said 'okay,'" she responded with more assurance. "Now, let's talk about the details of owning a dog and what that looks like."

Can you see how my wife did not expressly commit to getting a dog, yet she acknowledged and empathized with her son's desire to have a dog and invited further exploration of his proposal? Offering empathy and saying *okay* removed the anticipated rejection and kept both of their emotions calm while they continued discussing their differing perspectives.

**How does *Just Say Okay* reduce discord?** When we listen with consideration and then say *okay* to another's ideas, we insert a breathing space that increases our capacity to empathize and harmonize with the other person. A true story illustrates how this works. Connor came home from work one day and proudly announced to his family that they would be moving a thousand miles north to Wisconsin for his new job. Stunned by her husband's unforeseen declaration, but not wanting to fight in front of their children or immediately dismiss his career opportunity, Chloe took a deep breath and exclaimed, "Okay, dear…. Can we talk about this and what it would mean for our family?" With that bit of breathing space, Connor apologized, and they were able to discuss the unexpected announcement and civilly consider all the implications of the move. Despite Connor's thoughtlessness that created a tense moment, Chloe trusted her husband enough to consider that he may have made a good choice. She suppressed potentially negative emotions in her response by saying "okay," which allowed them to discuss the decision further without drama.

Connor had had his family's best interest in mind, and because of this experience, he learned to communicate with more care and consideration. Through their mutual respect and using *Just Say Okay* during a crucial interchange, they were able to suspend the potential fight and thoughtfully work through the sudden change of circumstances. The couple together chose to move, which turned out to be beneficial for their family—which eventually led to what they both really wanted.

> *Just Say Okay* inserts a momentary,
> emotional pause that allows logical
> progress to continue.

Another true story shows how *Just Say Okay* helps flip a switch from negative to positive emotions. The executive team of a company with which I worked decided to move to a new location about thirteen miles from their original building. One employee, Betty (name changed), hated the idea. She lived two miles from the original office, and she loved its proximity to her home. When Betty heard about the change, she was upset (negative emotion) and did not *want* her work location to move because she did not *want* to drive twenty-six miles every day to the new place. What she immediately *wanted* was to stay in the current location because it made her personal life easier. Betty made everyone aware of her desperate desire to stay in the old office, especially the executive team. Because of her upside-down condition, her coworkers steered clear of her. While her concerns about new commuting costs and distance were fair, her overly dramatic way of expressing frustration and refusing to consider the company's position were negative and toxic to others.

About two weeks after the announcement about the move, Betty took *The Invisible Four-letter Word* training. She learned about the interconnected nature of wants and how negative emotions and subsequent irrational conclusions affected her personally. Betty began to recognize that what she really wanted was to keep her job in a company she loved and that her upside-down behaviors were causing her to lose respect amongst her coworkers.

As she walked out of the seminar, Betty readily exclaimed, "Okay everybody, I'm ready to move!" Her coworkers stared at each other in disbelief. Practicing her new awareness, Betty had chosen to *Just Say Okay* to the company's move for the time being, and with her shift in tone, began regaining her respect by behaving more professionally in right-sided ways as she moved forward.

Another true experience illustrates the effect that *Just Say Okay* can have on conflict. I conducted an experiment with a group of teenagers. The instructions were simple: "When your mom or dad asks you to do something, just say *okay* and then do exactly what they request." This was a safe experiment because I already knew that these parents were full of consideration and would not take advantage of their teenagers.

After a few days, the youth reported the results. Some parents, when the teenager simply said *okay,* were confused by the odd response and continued to give instructions. Another parent paused in disbelief and then followed the teen to make sure he wasn't just saying *okay* and then ignoring the request. These parents were no doubt surprised by the unexpected response that defied stereotypical behaviors. Several of the teenagers shared that their parents began to treat them with more respect as they continued to practice the principle of *Just Say Okay*. They reported "feeling empowered" by this basic experiment.

An inability to say *okay* can lead to discord. A news story from November 18, 2016, figuratively illustrates this principle:

**Two Bull Moose Found Frozen in Mortal Combat**
by Brian Clark Howard

Two bull moose ended up locked in mortal combat forever, their final battle literally frozen in time. Two hikers found the animals encased in eight inches of ice in Alaska along the Bering Sea. "Two bulls got into a tussle over some ladies … and ended up being put on ice," said Jeff Erickson [moose photographer].[15]

Bill Samuel, a retired biologist and moose expert at the University of Alberta in Canada says he has never seen anything quite like it, though he is aware that the strength of the powerful animals and irregular shapes of their antlers can occasionally result in tangling the animals can't escape.[16]

This tragedy could have been avoided and death averted if one of the two moose had just figuratively said *okay* and walked away. Without conflict, the hypothetically considerate moose would have been able to meet another female moose. But because neither gave in nor paused the fight, the battle ended in death for both.

**Where else do we encounter forms of *Just Say Okay*?** In the field of clinical behavior analysis, *Just Say Okay* relates to concepts within experimental acceptance and commitment therapy.[17] *Accepting and committing* is an action-based approach that invites us to accept conflict and then commit to making changes in our behavior despite the discord and how we feel about it. It encourages individuals to develop psychological flexibility, which involves accepting difficult thoughts and emotions without trying to eliminate them but then taking committed action toward our most valued goals.[18]

For example, if I am presented with something I don't want (such as seeing police lights in my rearview mirror), I can choose to accept it in hopes of achieving what I really want. Eluding the police would quickly put me in a powerless position! So, I just say *okay* and pull my car over to the side of the road. My upright response to the officer might be, "Okay officer, I may have been speeding." In contrast, if I argue with her, the less likely it is that she will let me off with a warning. In my experience, when I have employed *Just Say Okay* in situations like this, I have been dismissed with a warning more times than I have been issued a ticket—which is what I really want.

A similar approach to *Just Say Okay* can be seen in a 2016 letter to amazon.com shareholders written by Jeff Bezos, the founder and CEO:

> Use the phrase "disagree and commit." This phrase will save a lot of time. If you have conviction on a particular direction even though there's no consensus, it's helpful to say, "Look, I know we disagree on this, but will you gamble with me on it? Disagree and commit?" By the time you're at this point, no one can know the answer for sure, and you'll probably get a quick yes. This isn't one way. If you're the boss, you should do this too. I disagree and commit all the time.
>
> Consider how much slower [the] decision cycle would [be] if the team had to convince me rather than simply get my commitment. Note what this example is not: it's not me thinking to myself, "Well, these guys are wrong and missing the point, but this isn't worth me chasing." It's a genuine disagreement of opinion, a candid expression of my view, a chance for the team to weigh my view, and a quick, sincere commitment to go their way.[19]

Can you see how the concept of "disagree and commit" is another way of cultivating consideration? It is akin to saying, "I am interested in what you have to say, so until I understand more, let's keep moving forward." Instead of immediate gridlock, emotional animosity, filibuster, and wasted time, let's *Just Say Okay*, or as Bezos recommends, "disagree and commit." Both methodologies disarm conflict and stimulate innovation.

**How can *Just Say Okay* lead to a powerful position?** Have you ever experienced the pleasure of offering an idea to your boss and she immediately embraced it with ease? Her thoughtful consideration inspired your future creativity and willingness to share. Often the mere practice of saying *okay* allows new insights to germinate for both parties. It's like opening a window to let in fresh air.

At first, saying *okay* can feel like a surrender or a position of weakness, but with a little practice, you'll discover that using this tool ultimately leads to a powerful position because it prevents emotional hijacking and thereby increases the opportunity to find more rational conclusions.

Sacrifice shapes and adds value to the human experience, but our culture of impatience and general affluence tends to despise this essential principle. Remember the baseball player we discussed earlier who laid down a sacrifice bunt? His willingness to say *okay* actually *united* him with his manager, and his momentary sacrifice ultimately won the game for his team. Saying okay by making the bunt made him the hero. The player's sacrifice elevated his future, strengthening honor and respect—and acted as an essential component of the valuable relationship he had with his coach and team.

The next time someone asks you to do something you don't want to do—but is making a fair and reasonable request—what could happen if you practice the convention and say *okay?* At first, *Just Say Okay* does feel like a surrender of control, which leads to uncertainty and explains why so many people have difficulty with it. We all want to be in control. However, by wisely giving up what we want now (in safe circumstances), our sacrifice grants us greater control over future opportunities.

Recall the traffic roundabout. If we just plow our way into the roundabout without yielding, the likelihood of getting into an accident dramatically increases, potentially putting us in a powerless position due to the consequences. Disregarding the yield sign also could cost additional time and money. We may have to confront the police, our insurance company, and other angry drivers. Saying *okay* is a form of yielding where we hesitate for a moment, analyze the situation, and then proceed when a safe opening appears. This temporary pause reduces the likelihood of a negative impact and opens the future to favorable opportunities, empowering us to arrive at the desired destination.

---

## Embrace the paradox of giving up power to become powerful.

---

In another application, saying *okay* is an essential component of any twelve-step recovery program such as Alcoholics Anonymous—a program that ultimately restores an individual's power of self-control. The course encourages reflection (consideration) and then admission of powerlessness over addictions (*Okay, I have an addiction.*). These programs then counsel participants to submit (say *okay*) to a "higher power," enabling them to overcome their addiction. They embrace the paradox of giving up power to become powerful.

**Can I really *Just Say Okay*?** We call timeouts in sports; we yield at intersections with yield signs, but we begrudgingly say *okay* in conflict. For some, it is easy to *Just Say Okay*. For others, it is more difficult. We all have different capacities for openness and varying degrees of willingness. But any form of willingness to reconsider our position injects hope for a positive outcome and to achieve what we ultimately want. To do that, both parties must share some form of confidence and trust in each other. Otherwise, it may be best to skip this convention of the Core all together and move on to one of the other conventions. We must be judicious about when to say *okay*.

The power of *Just Say Okay* lies in how we use it to overcome resistance, preserve relationships, and progress with momentum and positive energy toward our goals. The more experience we have with saying *okay*, the more comfortable we become with it.

**What is the bottom line?** The Core convention of *Just Say Okay* carries a bit of magic. Saying *okay* is simple and beautiful. Like pressing a pause button before a conflict begins, it can cancel out the effects of negative emotions that tend to lead to irrational conclusions. When we feel negative emotions rising within us, that is the moment to remember this fabulous phrase. If we are accustomed to arguing, we might need to unlearn our natural impulsive response and *Just Say Okay*. This convention also empowers us to fully consider others' perspectives as we evaluate all sides of a conflict civilly and respectfully.

Similar to navigating a roundabout, the word *okay* creates space for us to yield, observe, enter, then exit, all without incident. Ironically, greater influence and respect come to those who yield. It is not as hard as you might think. Try it—*Just Say Okay*.

## Connecting the Principles

Coming back to your personal conflict experience, consider:

- Is there enough trust and respect between you and the other person for you to use the *Just Say Okay* convention?

- How can you apply *Just Say Okay* to your personal conflict?

- What barriers may currently prevent you from using *Just Say Okay* as a tool to help maintain progress toward your goal?

## Adjust Your Distance

Think back to a fight you had with someone with whom you have a close relationship. Perhaps you knew you were right, and when they didn't listen to what you wanted, anger welled up within you. Then, you may have become irrational and even said something hurtful. Remember how that fight created distance in the relationship? Looking back now, you may wish you had handled it differently. If you had simply disengaged, walked away, cooled off, and let a little time pass, the outcome may have been more harmonious.

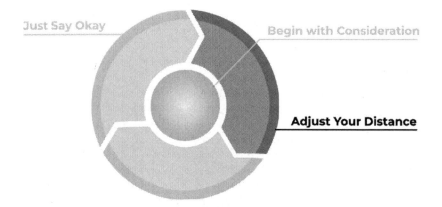

Just Say Okay

Begin with Consideration

**Adjust Your Distance**

The idea of disengaging from the emotional moment embodies The Core convention of *Adjust Your Distance*. A brief adjustment in proximity often prevents long-term regret.

**What does *Adjust Your Distance* look like?** Distance in this model represents the *time, space, and energy* between two people, objects, or events. It can be physical distance, emotional space, the distance of passing time, or the effort we exert. Our capacity to adjust distance is the key to understanding this principle—because to change the distance, the power to either increase or decrease that time, space, or energy must be in our control.

*Adjust Your Distance* requires us to consider our wants at the top of both the upright and upside-down pyramids. As we work through the process of prioritizing those wants, we can mindfully adjust distance to or from each of them.

To get closer to the things we want, we must concurrently get *away* from the things we *don't* want. To understand this principle better, consider this list of proactive adjustment examples:

- Getting away from friends who are a poor influence and moving closer to friends who inspire you to be better

- Getting away from things that are addictive and moving closer to things that empower you

- Getting away from time wasters and seeking things that are more worthwhile or intentionally relaxing

- Getting away from working too much and making time to nurture meaningful relationships

- Getting away from using company time to surf the internet and choosing to stay focused at work

- Getting away from things that cause negative emotions and choosing activities that create positive experiences

Adjusting distance entails turning around. If we are going in a direction we don't really want to go, we must stop, turn around, modify our course, and move toward our best and deepest desires.

The popular "start, stop, continue" feedback tool provides a method of applying the *Adjust Your Distance* principle.[20] The tool suggests making a list of things that you want to embrace—things to start doing. Then you make another list of things that you think you should stop doing because they prevent you from getting what you really want. Finally, create a third list of things to continue doing to progress toward a more powerful position.

The following scenarios help illustrate adjusting distance. Donovan felt frustrated about the amount of time his wife was spending with her friends. Instead of fighting with her when she got home, he got closer to her by making her favorite dessert. That action eased the tension and allowed them to discuss the matter civilly.

Jade was feeling financially burdened and needed more money for her living expenses. Instead of scrolling social media for hours each day, she decided to put her device in the closet and spend her newfound time starting a side business to supplement her income.

Mariah, a retail manager, witnessed a conflict between her employee and a customer who insulted the employee's service. Noticing the tension, Mariah waited until the customer left the store then listened to her frustrated employee' perspective with empathy. Instead of correcting how he dealt with the insulting customer, Mariah let the day pass so his emotions could settle. The next day, Mariah initiated a rational and constructive conversation about the previous day's negative episode.

**How does adjusting distance clarify our choices?** To effectively adjust our distance, we'll need to make conscious decisions and consider where each choice leads. Aristotle once said, "Nature abhors a vacuum." In other words, we can't just stop doing one thing then fail to fill the space with something else. People who stop smoking need to fill that void with something like chewing gum or sucking on a piece of candy as they transition habits. When we give up one thing, we need to replace it with another. Many good books, including *New York Times* bestseller, *The Power of Habit*, provide examples and details summarizing how and why we need to replace unwanted habits with others, which is a type of adjusting distance.[21]

Adjusting our distance enables us to see things from a slightly different vantage point. Sometimes we find ourselves in a time of life where we might dislike a coworker, a neighbor, a family member, our boss, or even our spouse. Perhaps we think divorce is the answer to our marital problems, but renewed romantic time might improve the marriage and prevent the unintended consequences that divorce creates. Maybe we want to quit our job, but an honest review with our boss would help adjust the needed distance to reduce our stress. Instead of giving an immediate rebuttal to a coworker's lofty proposal, perhaps you could apply a little consideration, say *okay*, or let a day pass before providing significant feedback. These adjustments usually move us closer to consensus, harmony, and respect while moving us away from conflict, dissonance, and dismissive attitudes.

> To get closer to the things we want,
> we must concurrently get away from
> the things we *don't* want.

Adjusting our distance means fine-tuning the position of the sliders within the Six Dimensions of Desire (chapter 3). During these stressful storms of life, could it be that we are too focused on ourselves? "I *want* more time alone." "I *want* freedom." "I *want* to be me." I want! I want! I want! If we really want to be right sided, we must control and manage our wants by adjusting our distance from unregulated, egocentric, obsessive, or unrealistic wants and make choices toward those things that matter most.

**What is the bottom line?** The Core convention of *Adjust Your Distance* regulates our actions by inviting us to get away from things we don't want while moving closer to things we do want. Remember that consideration encourages us to *stop* thinking exclusively about ourselves and *start* thinking generously about others. *Adjust Your Distance* means modifying sliders in the Six Dimensions of Desire to create a more effective path to what we want.

Practicing *Adjust Your Distance* helps develop refreshing new views and positive solutions. Instead of chopping through the dense jungle of upside-down feelings, we can adjust distance to get away from the thickets of things we *don't* want and begin walking a clearer, more harmonious path toward the things we *do* want.

## Connecting the Principles

How might you adjust your distance relative to your personal conflict experience?

- To what could you get closer?

- From what might you need to add distance?

- How could these decisions affect what you really want?

## Remember What You Really Want

The fourth tool of The Core is *Remember What You Really Want*. This convention solidifies and secures the transition from behaving in upside-down ways to responding with an upright attitude. We first *recognize* what we *really* want and then *remember* that desire so that it becomes the force that propels our choices.

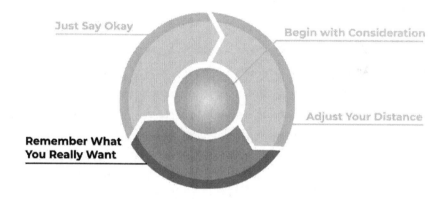

In 1996, the British pop band Spice Girls released their hit song "Wannabe." It has a catchy chorus about the invisible four-letter word:

Yo, I'll tell you what I want, what I really, really want
So tell me what you want, what you really, really want
I'll tell you what I want, what I really, really want
So tell me what you want, what you really, really want.[22]

Just like the song, this convention begs for a clear understanding of what we want. Once we know what we *really* want, then we can prioritize our actions and decisions based on those goals. Some examples include: Do we want to win the argument, or do we really want peace? Do we want to spend our money frivolously, or do we really want financial security? Do we want to build a cheap product, or do we really want to maintain our reputation as a quality company?

Remembering what we really want requires us to first *recognize* what we really want (the intentional want at the top of the upright pyramid) and then *remember* it when faced with an attractive alternative! Without this principle, it is difficult to ever attain the stability that comes from the upright powerful position. By remembering what we really want, we maintain our motivation and focus, even in the face of obstacles or challenges. Remembering what we *really* want solidifies our commitment to being more right sided.

**How does remembering *what* we want empower us to become *who* we really want to be?** Remembering what we really want requires the discipline to overcome the temptation to give in to short-term pleasures that hinder our long-term objectives. Mark Victor Hansen inspires us with this recommendation: "By recording your dreams and goals on paper, you set in motion the process of becoming the person you most *want* to be. Put your future in good hands—your own."[23]

So, what do you really want? Where would you like to end up? What are your goals? A plethora of excellent books exist on goal setting. Zig Zigler distills it down to one fantastic truth: "What you get by achieving your goals is not as important as what you *become* by achieving your goals."[24]

Consider taking some dedicated, focused time to ponder "what you want, what you really, *really* want." The process of writing goals down helps us identify and prioritize our many wants. Recording them also increases the odds of achieving them. By incorporating writing into our daily routines, we enhance our ability to remember and follow through with what we really want. The power of writing lies in its ability to engage our senses, organize our thoughts, and reinforce our memories.

What if you don't know what you really want? What if your life feels more like a moving target? Mental meandering or a feeling of emptiness can be signs of a missing purpose or that you face a crossroads. Asking heartfelt questions can help us clarify what we really want. Some examples for thoughtful analysis include:

- What are my specific goals?

- What are my most treasured desires for myself and my loved ones?

- How do my goals affect people around me or relate to the important relationships in my life?

- When would I like to have my goals accomplished?

- Do I want it like A or more like B?

- What am I willing to do or not do to accomplish my desires?

- What do I need to change in my current situation?

- Will I need to adjust my discipline, routine, or habits to obtain my objectives?

- Are my choices compromising any of my values, beliefs, or ethics?

- Where will my goals likely lead?

Remembering what we really want creates a constancy in purpose, which further leads to consistency in character.

**Why do we tend to forget?** Yes, the invisible four-letter word can affect our memories! If we don't *want* to do something or don't want to make a decision about it, we tend to easily forget it or dismiss it. For example: A wife is planning to go to her parents' house the next weekend and discusses it with her husband. He nods his head and utters the required *yeah, yeah, yeah* (he doesn't necessarily like his in-laws). He prefers (wants) to stay home and work on his car. When Saturday morning arrives, she begins packing the car and asks for help. Surprised, the husband responds,

"Wait, what? Where are we going?" Sometimes we may subconsciously forget things we just don't want to remember.

Similarly, it is possible to train ourselves to forget things. Lund University in Sweden researched memory and found that we can control forgetfulness.[25] In 2011, Gerd Thomas Waldhauser conducted neuroimaging studies where volunteers were asked to practice forgetting facts. Through EEG measurements, Waldhauser observed that the same parts of the brain were activated when suppressing a memory as when restraining a motor impulse. "We can, for example, rapidly instruct the brain not to catch a cactus that is falling from a table," the study says. If this is true, we can also instruct the brain to forget about awful projects our boss assigns us or household chores we disdain. The more often we suppress information, the more difficult it becomes to retrieve.

**What is the bottom line?** The act of remembering represents a powerful habit—we choose to remember those things we care about most and tend to forget what we care least about. Remembering requires both our minds and our bodies. Therefore, to *Remember What We Really Want* requires proactive actions. We must identify what we really want, then committing it to memory with writing, sharing, or making goals helps us act on it more consistently. When we put effort into remembering and acting on what we really want, we increase our chances for success and decrease the odds of forgetting.

So, whenever you are feeling a bit upside down, remember this twist on the Spice Girls principle, "Yo, remember what you want, what you really, really want!"

## Connecting the Principles

From your personal conflict experience, identify what you really want. Then consider the following:

- How does remembering what you really want alter your feelings about or perspective of the conflict?

- How does considering what you really want change how you will solve the conflict?

- What can you write down to help make what you *really* want a reality?

# Applying the Conventions of The Core

While the principles within the upside-down and upright pyramids make us aware of our wants, The Core provides four practical methods for regulating our response to our wants so we can transform upside-down thinking into upright action. These conventions help us to retrain and hone our problem-solving skills, develop better habits, address conflicting ideas and agendas, link us with others, and maximize a growth mindset. Using each tool requires thoughtfulness, action, and practice. Let's explore some examples of how these methods work collectively.

Rhett has a neighbor who owns a black Labrador. Wanting the dog to experience freedom, the neighbor frequently lets him out to wander the neighborhood unattended. Periodically, the lab comes into Rhett's well-manicured yard and does his duty, leaving an unwelcome package behind for Rhett's toddler to step in. When anger wells up within him over this issue, he feels a bit upside down. He *Begins with Consideration* by reminding himself his neighbor recently lost his wife and he wants to be a supportive neighbor.

He chooses *Adjust Your Distance* as his tactic because just saying *okay* doesn't really work for this situation. He practices patience, restraint, and tolerance by saying to himself, "Take some time to think about it." After his emotions subside, he rationally forms a plan to speak calmly with his neighbor.

Rhett could also begin with *Remember What You Really Want.* He understands his neighbor is going through a tough time, and he ultimately wants to maintain a peaceful relationship with him. He decides to buy some dog treats, offer them as a gift, and then discuss the matter civilly. Remembering his long-term desire for friendly neighbor relations enables Rhett to be prudent, responsible, and considerate. The conventions of The Core help transform Rhett from feeling upside down to being an upright neighbor.

The Core conventions also could help a couple follow the common advice to "never go to bed angry." Let's say you and your spouse are engaged in a heated argument about the kids. You decide to apply this counsel by staying up late to hash it out. As the hours wear on, you both become tired and subsequently more irrational. A likely ending could be hurt feelings and unkind words that aren't helpful or true, with no real resolution. Could it be better to *Just Say Okay* and then *Adjust Your Distance* by stopping the conversation until a better time? You can then begin a new day, revisiting the conflict with more consideration, a renewed perspective, and fewer emotional impairments.

---

Remembering what we really want creates a constancy in purpose, which further leads to consistency in character.

---

When you collect the courage to *Just Say Okay*, you reduce the risk of an emotionally charged, irrational conflict. The utterance of this simple word makes it nearly impossible for you and the other person to lock horns in an emotional, senseless battle that could lead to additional fighting. Proactively saying *okay* to the other person's argument extends a form of empathetic listening.[26] *Okay* introduces an emotional break so both of you can settle into a more rational state of mind and expand your power of persuasion later.

This break enables you to *Adjust Your Distance* by letting go for the moment and allowing time to pass, perhaps preventing regrets. Is it really a big deal—right here, right now?

As your mind gains composure, your ability to think rationally increases, and clarity comes, allowing both of you to recognize and *Remember What You Really Want*.

**Why is practical application important?** Successful transition from an upside-down state to a right-sided state of being requires physical action. Merely thinking *okay*, pondering distance, or contemplating what we really want are inadequate. Simply wrestling with The Core inside our heads is insufficient for stabilizing the metaphorical pyramid. Change demands action!

Studies have shown that the best way to control the brain is through the body.[27] We motivate ourselves by physically employing some of these Core tactics:

- Stand up straight and say *okay* out loud with positive posture.

- Get up and physically separate yourself from something.

- Call someone and tell them how you want to come closer to them.

- Invest in a journal and write down what you really want.

- Develop an action plan based on your written wants.

- Get up early and proactively follow your action plan.

- Make a list of the things you desire and why.

- Compose daily entries in your journal about the rewards you experience and the benefits you encounter each day.

- Offer praise to others and savor compliments you receive.

- Use breathing exercises to refresh your mind and body.

- Show consideration through gracious and courteous words and actions, such as saying please and thank you.

The four elements of The Core can help us create a strategic plan, but strategy without tactics is like a rocket without fuel. Our actions fuel the rocket as we look for opportunities to practice each concept. As we become proficient with the principles, we can land where we *really* want to be!

**Can people change direction?** Absolutely! None of us are the same person we were ten years ago. Change is inevitable: businesses change, family dynamics change, and public policies change. The good news is neuroscientists have discovered that when we decide to be receptive to change and accept the discomfort of uncertainty, our curiosity and learning receptors activate.[28] Essentially, discomfort fosters growth while comfort lulls us into stagnation and complacency. Embracing change isn't easy, but it's worth it. A willingness to change reduces conflict and enhances personal growth.[29] Time and experience transform us from within.

With practice, these four principles (*Begin with Consideration, Just Say Okay, Adjust Your Distance*, and *Remember What You Really Want*) can germinate a change within us. Like a caterpillar becoming a beautiful butterfly, this metamorphosis takes time, personal effort, and patience. We might be a little weak and wobbly at first, but time and tenacity reveal the beauty of transformation—and our confidence grows along with our honor and respect.

While it's always best to stay focused on your own personal transformation rather than trying to change someone else, sharing what you learn is a great way to reinforce it. John Seely Brown, a researcher who specializes in organizational studies said, "It's never enough to just tell people about some new insight. Rather, you must get them to experience it in a way that evokes its power and possibility. Instead of pouring knowledge into people's heads, you need to help them grind a new set of eyeglasses so they can see the world in a new way."[30]

With consideration as the new lens through which we view wants and how they relate to those around us, we can practice applying the four conventions until we realize the changes that we seek in ourselves. In thirty years, I have witnessed many people who changed their lives dramatically—those who really *wanted* to change.

**What if it feels too hard to change?** Sometimes we may need someone to help us through The Core. Right-sided transitions succeed more readily when we partner with respected mentors who are willing to help. We might look for someone who exhibits stable, confident, yet caring characteristics—someone we honor and respect. We can take that person's hand as they help us work toward big changes. Allowing them to be both coach and cheerleader, we can start with humility, accept the guidance they offer, and thoughtfully apply the tools described within The Core.

**What if someone asks us to help them change?** Sometimes we may be asked to help people who are in the most difficult circumstances of powerlessness. In these cases, those being helped must find the courage to accept these Core tools and trust their mentor. Mentoring requires courage and bravery because in all transformations, there will be success and failure, joy and sorrow, gratitude and grumbling, peace, and pain! Additionally, keep in mind that factors such as substance abuse, mental illness, or addiction make irrationality more likely, hindering progress and adding setbacks.

Recalling the story about Michael, the following excerpt from his own words depicts the courage it took to apply these principles as I helped him through his life changes:

> I was a drunken mess. Scott had taken me to his home to spend some time with his loving family and to detox. While there I opened up to them and shared with them little pieces of the true me. We laughed, loved, and played for two days. …I felt loved. I remember going through my belongings and giving away everything I didn't think was necessary.

I also remember Scott sitting me down and unfolding the plan he had for me. He told me that he would be taking me to San Francisco to a place called Delancey Street. He said that it was a facility that dealt with people who have similar issues as mine and that it would be a two-year commitment. My heart sank like a cannonball screaming through a bottomless shaft. My head in my hands, I knew that I couldn't do it. I also knew that at the pace I was going, the alternative was a swift departure from this world. Thoughts of the epic failure of past rehab programs flashed through my muddled brain, and I told him that I didn't think I could do it.

He reminded me of a few things in a way that only Scott could. He told me that I had more strength than I gave myself credit for. He told me that I had to trust him. He reminded me that I had given my word that I would just say *okay* to whatever he asked. After all, I had resigned from my job and given up my apartment on his word that he loved me and would never do anything to hurt me. I acquiesced— that is to say, I said, "Okay."

We left for San Francisco at about 5 a.m. that Monday morning. I packed a small duffle bag with some things (I wouldn't need any of it), and we were off. We passed the seemingly endless miles talking with each other. We spoke of the relationship we had built. We talked about writing a book. We sat in silence wondering what the future would hold for me. I wanted to jump out of the car and run, never stopping.

We crossed the Bay Bridge into San Francisco and exited onto the Embarcadero. Two blocks from the exit was the Delancey Street Triangle. We parked, said a prayer, and walked to find the entrance, but we only found a black iron gate with no signs and just a doorbell. As I looked into the facility, I thought that there was no way this could possibly be the place. It was way too nice. I was expecting some run-down buildings in the Tenderloin District. I rang the bell, and my life would forever be changed.

A young woman, neatly dressed, came to the gate and asked how she could help. I introduced myself and said that I would like to come in. She opened the gate and invited both Scott and me inside. When we reached the front office, she took my duffle bag and some basic information, after which she politely told me that I was not to speak to anyone—even Scott—that I was to sit on the bench to my left, and that I could read the material on the table in front of me. Scott was invited to sit in the comfortable chairs to the right of the door. We looked at each other, not really understanding how significant the moment was.

I had some idea that I was about to go through an intake process but didn't have a clue that it was an interview. I sat on that hard bench for what seemed like forever. My mind was reeling. I went from a quiet confidence that I was about to receive some sort of "treatment," to confusion and even panic. What would happen if I didn't get in? Where would I go? I had committed everything to this moment—and so had Scott. I had given most of my things away, quit my job, given up my apartment—what would I do? I started to think long and hard about the choices that had led up to my sitting on that hard bench.

I began to reflect on my life. In my mind, the thought hit me like a freight train that this was it. I wouldn't last another month. If I didn't get the help that I so desperately needed, I would be dead before Christmas. It was at that very moment that a man walked through the door and told me to follow him. Although he was dressed in a shirt and tie, I could tell that he was hardened. He looked to me like he had seen a thing or two. I got up, gave Scott a wink, and followed. Scott and I had no idea that it would be the last we would see of each other for the next ten months.

As I walked up a set of stairs to what would be an interview room, I was awestruck at the beauty of the place. Not a speck of dirt anywhere, no trash, beautiful plants—it looked like a mansion! I thought that for sure I was at the administration building and that upon completing the interview, I would be taken to the real facility, a facility that my broken-down life deserved: lights blinking down a dark hallway, grime and dirt everywhere, people lurking lifelessly, hopelessness and despair around every corner.

I couldn't have been more wrong.

I entered the interview room. There were three men in the room, all dressed in shirts and ties. My heart was in my throat. I couldn't have felt more uncomfortable. One of the men had a clipboard and obviously seemed in charge. Even though he was dressed professionally, he looked hard, like he could have just come from prison. I felt intimidated. He asked me why I was there. Why had I come to Delancey Street?

Given that I didn't really know much about the place, I told the men that I needed help. I told them that I couldn't live my life on my own, that given the course that I was on, there was no way that I would make it. I told them that I had ruined nearly all my relationships as a result of my drug and alcohol abuse, and that I couldn't go on living the way that I had been. They asked me to leave the room. One of the men escorted me out into the hall to a chair and told me to sit. I did. I was starting to panic. Had I said something wrong? Certainly, I needed the help, but had they already decided that I wasn't Delancey material?

After what seemed like forever, probably five minutes or so, one of the men came back out of the room and asked me to come back in. He seemed to be put out. He told me to sit back down. I did. The man with the clipboard asked me to tell him my story. I began with the most horrible parts of my life. My thinking was that if they heard how hard my life was and how bad off I was, that surely, they would let me in. After having gone through some of my story, they asked me to go out in the hall and sit in the chair again. I was starting to sweat. The gravity of the position that I had put myself into was really starting to settle in.

My thoughts started to change. The intensity of the moment came in the thought that I wasn't asking to be let into a "program." I was begging, pleading for my life. A few moments passed, and I was invited back into the room. The energy in the room changed. What was, for a brief moment, empathy for the life that I had led, turned to disdain. The questions turned to what seemed like judgments. How could I have turned away from the people that loved and cared about me? How could I choose drugs, alcohol, and women over my loving wife and my beautiful boys? How could I be so selfish and self-centered? What made me so special that I was entitled to act so terribly in life and expect everyone around me to pick up the shattered pieces? I was bawling.

Fact is, I knew they were right. I just didn't have the strength to turn things around for myself—poor me. I still wasn't thinking of anyone but myself. At that moment I would have said or done anything to get in through those doors. What I did say was more of an acknowledgment of what a piece of crap I really was. That I wanted to change my life and that I would do anything they asked of me to do. It was at that moment that I realized I would have to give up what I thought was control over my life and give it to the hands of complete strangers.

It was different than just saying *okay* to Scott. I trusted Scott. I loved Scott. I knew that he only had my best interests at heart and that he wouldn't ever do anything to hurt me. Other than my sister, Scott was the only person I can honestly say that I trusted. I realized at that moment that if I was to survive, and possibly even change, I would have to place my trust in complete strangers.

The men reluctantly decided to accept me into Delancey Street. I was afraid. I still had no idea what that meant. Part of me sighed with relief, but part of me lacked anything resembling confidence that I would last five minutes (let alone two years) in that place.

I didn't get to say goodbye to Scott. I thought about how happy he must have been that they let me come in. I imagined the sigh of relief he must have felt that I was no longer his problem. I even started to get angry. Can you imagine? I was actually angry, thinking that he dropped me off here so that he wouldn't have to "deal" with me anymore. That's how messed up my mind was. He had taken a huge risk bringing me to Delancey Street, and all I could think was that I had once again been abandoned. Again, poor me!

From the moment Mimi Silbert decided to let me in and give me a chance, I began to change. I didn't understand anything that was happening—I didn't have to. In my mind, I believed that I was at the end of my rope. Little did I know that my life was only just beginning.

On the way to San Francisco, Scott and I had talked about how it would be for me. We talked about how I had so much to offer, that I would be able to help everyone around me. We were so wrong. It was I who would be helped, and it was everyone around me that had so much to offer. From the moment I arrived, I was floored with absolute humility. I instantly recognized that I was surrounded by strength. I came to see that perhaps my life wasn't so bad after all. I immediately decided that I would be brave, do everything asked, that I would just say *okay* a million times over.[31]

Michael's story illustrates his willingness to apply the conventions of The Core, exemplifying the courage and humility necessary to begin real change. The process of transforming unregulated, upside-down wants to upright, regulated choices utilizes these four Core tools as the catalysts for change. We *Begin with Consideration*, realizing that no specific order dictates the application of the other three conventions. To insert a pause when negative emotions arise, *Just Say Okay*. However, if the house is on fire, we don't *Just Say Okay* and let the building burn around us. We *Adjust Our Distance* by quickly getting out! In other situations, we may need to *Remember What We Really Want* before we can *Just Say Okay* or even *Adjust Our Distance*. Every situation differs and requires judgment and wisdom as we choose which tools best fit the situation.

The beauty of The Core lies in the combination of principles that work together to establish mutual understanding—through practice, patience, and careful application.

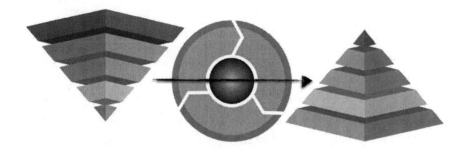

The Core is all about *becoming*. These four principled conventions strengthen and empower us to willingly lay aside our upside-down wants and champion with consideration our upright wants that refine us to become strong, stable, and honorable.

# The Worst Conflicts

What about serious conflict where the parties refuse principles of The Core—those who cannot or will not implement consideration for opposite views?

What if my wants and the wants of another person are mutually exclusive, meaning both cannot be satisfied at the same time?

What if neither opposing party *wants* to solve the conflict? Or only one of the two cares to find a solution?

These powerful questions highlight the fundamental dispute between the Jews and the Palestinians. They describe the battle between pro-choice and pro-life, the causes for contention between the political far right and the far left.

So, is there any way those divided factions can ever find consensus? This question is so substantial it requires another tool. The Core is designed to transform our responses to our wants, to transition us from upside down to right-side up. But mutually exclusive, conflicting wants require a different approach. A detailed examination of conflict reveals an assortment of answers and some interesting solutions for solving seemingly impossible contention.

Let's rephrase the question like this: *can serious conflict between two opposing wants really be resolved?* The focus of the next chapter is to answer this question and present a tool for resolving painful disputes.

CHAPTER 8

# RESOLVING CONFLICT

*"Conflict cannot survive without your participation."*

—Wayne Dyer

Humans have endured conflict since the beginning of recorded history. Adam and Eve had a fracas over the fruit. Cain and Abel fought over flocks—and those simply mark the beginning of conflict! Divisions, competitions, clashes, wars, and selfish wants have increasingly worsened since then. You want one thing; your partner wants something else.

Can conflict really be resolved? Is there a possibility to discover common ground? Can mutual understanding and harmony materialize from disputes? Can both opposing parties emerge with respect? How can you simply say *okay* to something you really don't want? What if two wants cannot coexist because they are mutually exclusive? Some scenarios underscore all of these questions, such as what if your spouse wants to live in San Diego and you want to live in Anchorage? What if your daughter wants a cat, but you are allergic to cats?

The answer to most of these questions depends on whether or not both parties *want* to solve the disagreement. With a willing heart, any controversy *can* be resolved. While your wants get you into conflicts, only your wants can get you out of them.

## What Makes Conflict Real

Yes, conflict is everywhere—including inside our own heads. Examples include divorce, money management disputes, lawsuits, drama and corruption in the workplace, physical fights between people, wars between nations, political divisions, rebellious children, and the list goes on. Conflict is ubiquitous.

That said, Eliyahu M. Goldratt, author and creator of the Theory of Constraints,[1] audaciously declared: "There are no conflicts in reality."[2] How could he say such a thing? I have pondered this statement for years. While controversial, it contains a powerful truth. The key to his statement is "in reality." Let's examine that more closely.

Chinese communist leader Mao Zedong said the exact opposite of Goldratt: "Contradiction is universal, absolute, existing in all processes of the development of things and running through all processes from beginning to end."[3] Dr. Goldratt and Chairman Mao take extreme, opposite positions. One is a capitalist, the other a communist. No wonder they have such different views! Between these two extremes sits an insightful quotation from King Charles III. He said:

> Conflict, of course, comes about because of the misuse of power and the clash of ideals…. But it also arises, tragically, *from an inability to understand, and from the powerful emotions* which, out of *misunderstanding*, lead to distrust and fear[4] (italics added).

Note the key concepts in King Charles' statement. If this is true, then conflict comes from misunderstanding, which arises either from lack of full information or powerful negative emotions. Both lead to irrational or false conclusions, which indicates that conflicts of this nature are indeed imagined, untrue, or fabricated.

When Goldratt says that conflicts don't exist *in reality*, his assertion is true because erroneous assumptions are *not based on factual reality*. Interestingly, Chairman Mao is also correct in his statement. Of course, contradiction is universal because false assumptions are also universal. The capitalist and the communist seem to agree!

*To assume* means to take for granted or believe without proof. Assumptions show others that we have put our thinker in the stinker! False assumptions amount to thoughtlessness because they are not based on a factual foundation or a logical thinking process.

King Charles' statement infers that if *understanding* (and thoughtfulness) can be cultivated, conflict will give way to a strengthened relationship rather than a weakened one.[5] Remember, in the upright pyramid, harmony is at the apex of a person's life. When two people respect each other, conflict diminishes. So, is the combination of *misunderstanding* and *negative emotions* the root cause of all conflict? When caught in a conflict, I sometimes stop and ask myself, "Am I living in the real world, or have I wandered into the false assumption world?"

If we eliminate false assumptions that occur when we forget to "seek first to understand," we disarm *most* conflicts, or we find a solution that considers both sides. I am not asserting that conflicts don't exist, but that no conflicts exist in reality *that can't be solved.*

When taking an upright approach, developing rational conclusions and seeking common ground can dissolve discord. One such example is the creation of the United States Constitution, which was fiercely debated but resulted in the profound establishment of a new government. This was possible because the representatives from the various states passionately debated their ideas with a common goal in mind, which was to establish a constitution that could be accepted by all states to govern the new country. Once that *shared goal was understood and defended* within the conflict, that unity for their goal enabled them to move forward—and ultimately made a successful outcome possible.

## An Interpersonal Conflict Story

Let's look at a specific interpersonal conflict and then analyze its underlying assumptions.

"Ugh! That jerk!" Kayla blurted aloud as she slammed the steering wheel with the palms of her hands. Her emotions were steaming like a bowl of soup. The empty driveway clearly proved that her husband, Alan, wasn't home yet. That's what sparked her anger. She slammed the car into park before it came to a stop.

Kayla forcefully put her shoulder into the car door as she opened it. It flew wide open then sprung back with such force that the window hit her in the head. A nasty four-letter word shot from her mouth.

Once inside the house, she threw her keys across the room and cringed as they hit a picture frame on the wall, breaking the glass and knocking the frame to the floor.

"I'm done!" she exclaimed.

Plopping down on the couch, Kayla began to cry. It was Friday night, and what she really wanted was a night out with Alan. After a terrible week at work, she needed a break.

Alan had promised to come home early so they could go to dinner and a movie. Now, here she sat at six forty-five, alone and stressed out, with no husband to take her away.

*Did he completely forget about me? What if he went out drinking with his buddies?* she mused to herself with clenched teeth and folded arms. *I wanted to go out, and he left me high and dry again! Where the hell is he?* she fumed in her head while holding back tears.

Kayla pulled her phone out of her pocket and tapped to call him. She flung her hair back, wiped her cheeks, checked the time, and then put the phone back to her ear. Her emotions were on red alert.

"Hellooo, Babe," Alan answered coyly.

"Where are you?" she demanded with daggers.

"I'm just leaving work," he said, his tone now defensive.

"You should have left forty minutes ago!" she demanded.

"Listen, honey, I had a last-minute call from a customer who needed the tracking number for a missed delivery."

"I don't care about your customer. Did you forget we were going out tonight?"

"I didn't forget. I found the tracking number, so I'll be right—"

"Whatever!" she said as she hit the end button, cutting him off midsentence.

Kayla's mind was racing. *I'll show him! He can't treat me like that. He promised to take me out tonight! How insensitive can he be?* Her thoughts were like a loaded freight train barreling down the tracks, full steam ahead.

Angrily, she schemed, "I'll make my own dinner. He can fend for himself!"

Kayla shuffled to the kitchen, where she opened the refrigerator door and pulled out a bag of pre-mixed salad and a container of cottage cheese. She grabbed a bag of croutons from the cupboard. After mixing it in a glass bowl, she stabbed a fork in the middle of it several times, imagining it was Alan.

"Ah, sweet satisfaction," she gloated as she left the kitchen with her dinner in hand. Kicking off her shoes, she flung them into the middle of the dining room.

*I hope he trips on them*, she smirked, as she walked barefoot through the house to their bedroom, closing and locking the door behind her.

Kayla scooped up several pillows, made a cozy nest in the middle of the bed, and wiggled into a comfortable position. Slowly and deliberately, she ate her dinner, listening to the crunch of crispy vegetables and croutons. About halfway through the salad, she heard Alan's truck rumble up to the front of the house. His tires screeched to a stop. Within seconds, the front door swung open, then closed with a thud. Kayla heard the tromping of his boots moving through the house.

"Kayla?" Alan's voice cried out in concern. "Kayla?"

She held her breath in silence.

"Kayla, honey, where are you?" she heard him plea in a distant part of the house.

She stopped chewing, as if it would give away her position, and sat in silence, her heart pounding loudly.

Alan's steps came close to the bedroom door. The doorknob jiggled.

"Kayla, baby, come on—let's go out. The night is still young. It's only seven," he coaxed softly through the locked door.

She restrained herself from responding. *He needs to feel my pain.* "Come on, honey," Alan pleaded. "Don't do this."

She sat firm. There was no way on earth she was going to budge. *He hurt me again*, she justified. *And now he's going to pay for it. I'm gonna win this battle, not him.*

She remained locked inside the bedroom, free from his careless choices.

## Analyzing the Assumptions

To seek a better understanding of the root cause of their conflict, let's analyze the struggle between Kayla and Alan. While it appears that Kayla's wants formed the foundation of this battle, was there more to the conflict than that?

Instead of looking at each individual's wants, let's examine what Kayla *thought* or *supposed*—either of which amounts to an assumption.

First, Kayla judged Alan to be a jerk. He obviously had hurt her in the past, but regardless of the history, assuming the worst in the heat of the moment only fueled her negative emotions. Her assumptions initiated feelings of hostility. These negative emotions led to irrational thoughts, and those ideas ignited additional assumptions. She was barreling down the wrong path.

"I'm done!" Kayla exclaimed. Was she really done? Was there no energy left for what she really wanted? What if Alan's car had broken down? What if he was in an accident? What if he had stopped to buy her flowers? Would she still be "done!"? Her negative emotions hijacked her ability to think clearly, and in this commandeered condition, her erroneous assumptions intensified the battle and left little room for consideration.

Next on the list of Kayla's thoughts was, *I'll bet he went out drinking with his buddies and forgot about me.* But we know from the content of the story that Alan had not forgotten about her.

We could go on to psychoanalyze what *she* should have done and what *he* should have done, but that's not the point of this exercise; our focus is on the root cause of conflict. We have identified that Kayla had three thoughts, all based on false assumptions that caused contention between her and Alan. The crazy thing was, up to this point in her thinking process, Alan hadn't even been there to participate in the conflict!

Was there a conflict *in reality*, or was it all in Kayla's head? She reacted to her own conclusions, proclaiming herself done and locking herself in their bedroom—even though no one physically was present to fight with her.

Internal strife based on erroneous assumptions is exhausting! *False assumptions are the root cause of most conflicts.* John Steinbeck brilliantly explains, "All war is a symptom of man's failure as a thinking animal."[6]

False assumptions flourish when we don't get what we want. Sprinkle in some negative emotions, and our minds conjure up all kinds of fictitious stories. That is when most conflicts erupt.

The quotation on the first page of this chapter by Wayne Dyer, American self-help author and motivational speaker, sums it up: "Conflict cannot survive without your participation." So, let's take a proactive approach to put an end to conflict!

## The Consensus Diagram

Archimedes, the Greek mathematician, declared, "Give me a lever long enough and a fulcrum on which to place it, and I shall move the world."[7] Resolving conflict presents a monumental task that requires a specialized tool.

To be clear, an effective tool to resolve conflict does *not* seek a compromise. Juhani's Law states that "A compromise will always be more expensive than either of the suggestions it is compromising." [8]

Compromise leaves both parties feeling dissatisfied with the outcome, whereas a *win-win* solution empowers both parties, helping them feel emotionally fulfilled and satisfied by the results. Yet, finding a win-win solution is no easy task; the effort involves unbiased consideration. But as Einstein is believed to have said, "Problems cannot be solved by the same level of thinking that created them."[9]

If we need new thinking and want to discover truth, and if erroneous assumptions lie at the heart of conflict, what must we do to expose those falsehoods and invite open-mindedness? How can we eliminate convoluted thinking and initiate rational considerations?

---

## While your wants get you into conflicts, only your wants can get you out of them.

---

Goldratt developed what he called the Evaporating Cloud Diagram.[10] His five-block blueprint identifies and clarifies the underlying arguments of conflict, then exposes the associated assumptions. I have modified Goldratt's original concept to fit the principles within *The Invisible Four-letter Word*. Business professionals might call this a negotiation tool, but I simply entitle it *The Consensus Diagram*. The Consensus Diagram helps nurture agreement and harmony between conflicting people or ideas.

A familiar fable, "The Three Little Pigs" works well to demonstrate the Consensus Diagram. The pigs lived as productive members of their fictional society, just trying to get along in life. Then, a big, bad wolf began to terrorize their world. The wolf *wanted* to eat the pigs and the pigs didn't *want* to be eaten. That defines the conflict. The Consensus Diagram exposes the inherent assumptions in the story and seeks to identify a win-win solution for both parties.

Here I need to stop and offer a word of warning. Be cautious when using this tool between you and another person to work out your personal conflict because it is difficult to convince others of your position when you might be making false assumptions yourself. You may need to use a third-party mediator, such as a friend, family member, or your boss, to ensure your rationale and the other person's logic are sound. If your conclusions are in any way irrational, then you only impair your own honor and respect. It's easy for either party to accuse the other of being upside down, which undermines the efficacy of The Consensus Diagram.

Because the Consensus Diagram's steps and process help expose potential false assumptions on both sides of the conflict, they need to be explored in an unbiased way. For that reason, the process below is described from a mediator's point of view. If you or anyone else acts as the mediator, or if you are attempting to resolve your own conflict, remember that *you must remain unbiased and non-judgmental, without taking sides.*

Additionally, you can use this tool in a mediation role to help just one person if the conflict is between them and their own wants or between them and society. For example, you can use it to assist a person struggling with substance abuse, a disgruntled employee, or anyone who is open and willing to receive help. To use this tool to resolve a personal, inner conflict, the person answers the same questions but for each side of their conflict.

The seven steps of The Consensus Diagram include:

1.  Discover if both parties want to solve the problem.

2.  Ask each party to clearly specify what they want.

3.  Find out why each party wants what they want.

4.  Identify the shared want.

5.  Verify each parties' statement.

6.  Test each assumption.

7.  Craft a solution.

## Step 1. Discover if both parties *want* to solve the problem.

The first task for overcoming conflict is to identify if the people involved are trending upside-down or upright, then *ensure they are both ready to solve the disagreement before moving forward*. Look at the pyramid models to see if either party fits one side or the other. Are they displaying negative emotions? Are they making irrational statements? Are they reactively responding with closed body language or other indicators of resistance? Do both parties want to solve the problem? (NOTE: While the parties disagreeing may or may not understand the pyramids, the mediator needs to understand the pyramid indicators enough to evaluate the parties' readiness to solve the problem.)

**What to do:** If either one of them is feeling upside down and isn't motivated to solve the conflict, do not attempt to resolve the strife. You might start by verifying their willingness to work toward a solution. "I can see that you may not be ready to discuss this issue. Would there be a better time?" If either party doesn't express a willingness to solve the problem, then employ The Core principle of *Adjust Your Distance*. Allow them some time and space to calm their feelings. Plan a future opportunity to solve the problem when there is a greater chance for positive emotions and rational conclusions. When that time comes, then ask them, "Would you be willing to consider solving ...?" then add the conflict at hand.

Only when both parties verify their willingness to solve the problem should you proceed to step 2.

**Case study illustration:** Let's assume the three little pigs have an upright attitude and are willing to solve the problem.

I begin, "Piggies, do you want to solve the conflict you are having with the wolf?"

"Yes," they reply with eagerness. "We'll do anything to make peace with that guy. Our lives are horrible right now. We live in terror inside our brother's brick home."

I turn to the Big, Bad Wolf and ask, "Mr. Wolf, would you like to resolve this conflict you are having with the pigs?"

"I'm not sure if there is a conflict," responds the wolf. "If they won't come out, I'll just climb down the chimney. They can't stay in there forever."

It doesn't seem like the wolf is open to a win-win solution. I need to see if he is willing to increase his consideration. If not, I'll have to temporarily close the case on this rivalry (*Adjust Your Distance*) and come back another time when he is more open.

But, before giving up, I press further by asking, "Would you be willing to consider a better solution than all this huffing and squeezing down chimneys? I mean, you could overexert yourself or get stuck in the chimney or worse.... Are you open to other options?"

Leaning back for a moment, the wolf reluctantly answers, "I guess I could do that. What's there to lose? I'm just sitting around waiting for them to come out anyhow."

We all have moments of lucidity even when we are feeling upside down. Because the wolf is open to rational solutions, which fits the upright pyramid, we can move to step 2.

## Step 2. Ask each party to clearly specify *what* they want.

This step helps *each party discover and articulate what they specifically want.* We will apply this want to the first box within the framework of the Consensus Diagram, which is divided into three sections. Labeled from left to right, the diagram's three sections include the wants, whys, and common want. These comprise the primary elements of the Consensus Diagram.

## <u>Consensus Diagram:</u>
### Conflicting Wants

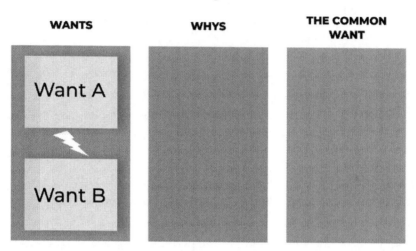

**What to do:** On the left section under *Wants*, place two sticky notes or draw two squares one above the other. Ask each person to clearly explain what they *want*. See if you can identify why both wants cannot be satisfied at the same time. Describe the wants as specifically and concisely as possible based on what each party explains, ensuring they are *mutually exclusive*; this means implementing one want would rule out the other. (This tool focuses on the extreme opposition of wants; when opposing wants aren't mutually exclusive, they are easier to resolve and don't require use of this tool.)

Write each want as a complete sentence. When both wants are recorded, draw a lightning bolt between the two sticky notes symbolizing the rift between the wants. Ask each party if this diagram accurately defines the conflict. Keep the discussion going until you get full agreement from both sides that they are happy with what is written.

**Case study illustration:** Let's go back to the pig and wolf story.

"Little pigs, tell me what you want," I say.

"We don't want to be eaten."

"That's it?" I ask.

"Yep. Pretty simple," they respond.

I write on the top sticky note (Want A): *We don't want to be eaten.* Then I turn to the wolf and ask, "What do you want?"

"Bacon!" he exclaims voraciously. The poor little pigs gasp in horror as the wolf snickers, exposing his long, white teeth.

"Bacon, eh?" I calmly respond, trying to reassure the pigs. "Is that it? Just to be clear, you want bacon. Is that right?"

"Yep, that's right," the Wolf replies without making eye contact.

"Well then, that's what I'll put down on note B." I write *I want to eat bacon* on the sticky note and notice the poor little pigs are clinging to each other and shuddering in their hooves.

## Consensus Diagram Example:

### Conflicting Wants Defined

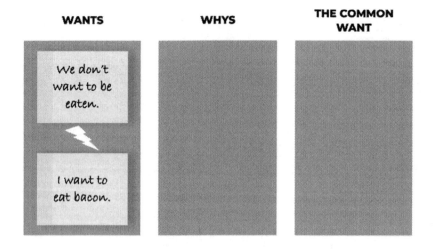

## Step 3. Find out *why* each party wants what they want.

In step 3, the goal is to *identify why each party wants what they want*, which will be written in squares in the center section.

**What to do:** Add two sticky notes or draw squares to the center section, one to the right of Want A and one to the right of Want B. Ask each person *why* they want what they want and remind them to be specific. Again, write each answer in a full sentence, and be as concise and clear as possible. Draw a "logical line" linking the want sticky notes with their respective why answers. (We will come back to these significant lines later.)

### <u>Consensus Diagram:</u>
Rationales

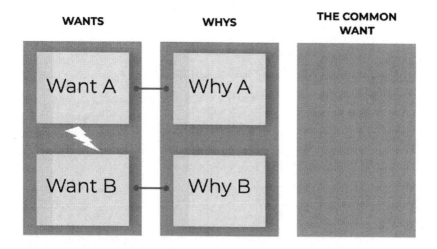

**Case study illustration:** We revisit the conflicted animals.

"Piggies, can you please tell me why you don't want to be eaten?" I ask.

"Isn't it obvious?!" they cry out. "We want to live!"

Nodding in total agreement, I write *We want to live!* on the top-center note and reassure them with a smile. "That's a good answer."

The wolf can't wait for his turn, and while clapping, he blurts out his answer, "I love bacon!"

"Fair enough," I say, writing *I love bacon* on the bottom-center note. "Does that sound good to everyone?" I ask for confirmation (not realizing *good* could be misconstrued with *bacon*).

"Sounds great!" responds the wolf with a broad smile on his face as he licks his lips. The poor pigs look petrified.

The updated Consensus Diagram now appears like this:

## Consensus Diagram Example:

### Rationales Defined

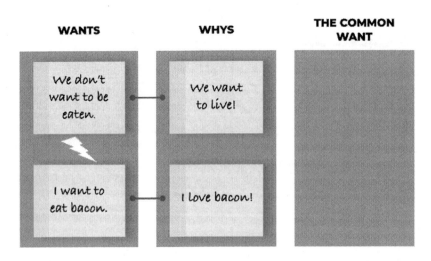

|  WANTS | WHYS | THE COMMON WANT |
|---|---|---|
| We don't want to be eaten. | We want to live! | |
| I want to eat bacon. | I love bacon! | |

## Step 4. Identify the *shared want*.

In step 4, we *identify the common want* each side desires in the argument. This step in the Consensus Diagram is an interesting one because we can't have a conflict unless a shared want or a common objective exists. Without a mutual want, the two parties go their separate ways.

For example, a couple going through a divorce spends time and money over the custody of their daughter. She is the shared want. But what if the father doesn't care about custody of the child? What if he doesn't really *want* to spend time with his daughter? There would be no need for a debate or custody battle. The mother would be awarded custody, and the father would keep the freedom he is looking for. Without both parties wanting custody of the daughter (the common objective), there is no conflict. The battle doesn't exist.

To resolve disagreements, the shared want must be clearly identified. Sometimes this can be difficult to determine, but remember, unless there is a common objective, there is no conflict! The common want helps reveal the false assumptions within the conflict.

**What to do:** The best way to find the common want is to apply one of The Core principles when you ask: what do you *really* want? Encourage each side to look beyond current circumstances and describe what they are *looking for* in the long term.

Next, help them identify what they really want by having them finish this statement: "I really want (A) because...." Give them time to answer; the goal is to draw from each party what they really want. You can also ask "why" questions, looking for the rationale. "Why do you want (A)?"

## Consensus Diagram:
### Shared Want

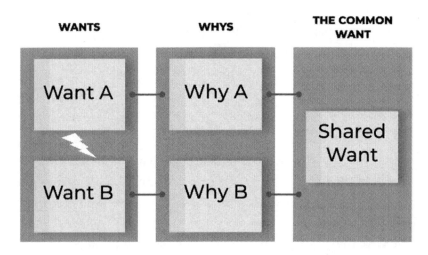

You may have to repeat this questioning process multiple times to drill down to the most basic wants driving the debate, which leads to discovery of the legitimate common objective. The final answer to this in-depth investigation must be the same from both parties.

**Case study illustration:** The conversation between the callous wolf and the frightened piggies continues with my questions.

"Piggies, what do you really want?" I ask.

"We want to stop running from house to house," they explain.

I take their answer and use it for the next question. "Why do you want to stop running from house to house?"

"Because we are running out of houses to run to!" they exclaim.

That answer becomes the basis for my next question. "Why are you running out of houses?"

"Because the wolf is relentless!"

"Why is he so relentless?" I inquire.

"I DON'T KNOW!!" squeals the bricklayer pig. "Why are you asking us so many questions?! Ask him!"

To alleviate the tension, I hold up my hands and say, "Okay, okay." Turning to the wolf, I continue with the previous answer from the pigs. "So, why are you so relentless in chasing the pigs?"

The wolf ponders for a moment then reveals, "Because I am hungry."

Using the same pattern, I ask the next obvious "why" question. "Why are you so hungry?"

"Because I keep chasing those dang pigs all over the countryside!"

"Is that what you really want, Mr. Wolf?"

"NO! I would rather have a nice sit-down meal—one that doesn't take so much running around."

This is where I pay careful attention. I notice the wolf would rather enjoy eating a sit-down meal *over* running around chasing his dinner. Those are two different wants!

**What to do (continued):** This is the point where you need clarification to find the common objective. In other words, when you hear the opposite of what has been said or has been happening, seize that idea and then ask for more clarification.

**Case study illustration:** I dig a little deeper with the wolf.

"You would *rather* have a sit-down meal? Help me understand that a little more."

The wolf sits back in his chair, squints his eyes, and ponders for a moment before replying, "I *would* like to eat without all the huffing and puffing. I'd like to eat in peace."

As a token of affirmation, I gently nod my head, smile at the wolf, and say, "Thank you for your honesty."

Turning back to the pigs, I press, "Let's go back to the previous questions. You told me what you didn't want. You didn't want the wolf chasing you from house to house because you were running out of houses. Now tell me what you *do* want."

"We don't want to have to run around all of the time."

I shake my head. "No, I didn't ask what you don't want. I asked what you *do* want."

"We want to live in our homes in peace," they concluded.

With this answer, I discover that both the pigs and the wolf stated that they want peace. It looks like the common want has been revealed.

**What to do (continued):** Next, clarify the common objective just discovered. The synonymous answer from the interrogation goes on a single sticky note or in the square to be applied to the section on the right. Be sure to write the common want in a complete sentence, and then connect the box back to Why A and Why B with two more "logic lines" that will be used to induce rational thinking in step 6.

**Case study illustration:** I ask the animals, "Pig brothers, what do you *really* want at the end of all this?"

"We want to live our lives. We want peace—without the fear of the wolf eating us!"

"Completely reasonable," I say. "What do you really want in the end, Mr. Wolf?"

"I want to be happy, too. I want to be full, satisfied, and not have to chase those slippery swine all over the place."

I scratch my head at this contradiction and ask for further clarification, looking for the identical want.

"I guess I want contentment," the wolf replies.

Turning to the pigs again, I ask, "Is that what you want, too?"

"Yes! Contentment, peace. We want the same thing. We just want to live our lives without having our houses blown down. We want peace of mind."

Turning back to the wolf, I inquire, "If your stomach were full, would that give you what you are looking for? Would that give you peace of mind? Is peace of mind what you *really* want?"

"Yes!" responds the not-so-big or bad wolf.

"Okay then, your shared want is *We want peace of mind*."

## Consensus Diagram Example:
### Shared Want Identified

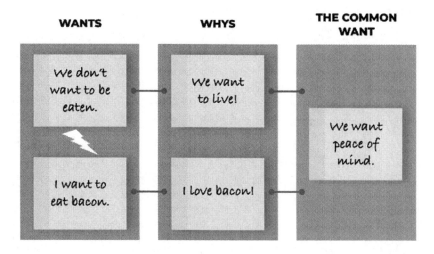

## Step 5. Verify each parties' *statement.*

In this step, we *verify the accuracy of both parties' statements* and confirm consensus. We must ensure that no one feels like they have been tricked, forced, or coerced into agreeing with what has been written. Neither party should feel like they had words put in their mouths, or that they were blackmailed or railroaded in any way. Everyone must willingly agree that the statements in the Consensus Diagram are true and voluntary.

**What to do:** Ask each party if the written statements are true and confirm that they agree with each of them.

**Case study illustration:** I verify each statement written in the diagram with the animals. The pigs nod their heads in unison while the wolf confirms, "Yeah, looks good," with a dismissive wave of his paw.

## Step 6. Test the *assumptions*.

Remember the connecting lines linking the sticky notes or squares? Those "logic lines" represent the *underlying assumptions* between the statements.

The logic lines between ideas are begging for proof. These lines represent the assumptions between each statement that need validation to determine whether the assumptions are true or false. Spurious expectations provide the breeding ground for false assumptions.[11] We must examine each link to ensure the assumptions between the statements are rational or irrational.

Importantly, more than one rationale can be found within each logic line. We can write as many connections as the person willingly reveals (logical or illogical). Rather than judging the responses, we simply write them down. The lines between the whys and the common objective generally have the fewest assumptions, whereas the connections between the wants and the whys often have the most. At least one assumption should be noted between each sticky note.

People usually know *what* they want, but the logical connection between what they want and *why* they want it can go unanalyzed. Careful consideration of those assumptions helps establish objectivity.[12]

**What to do:** To find the hidden assumptions within each line, use the word "because." For example, you might say, "You want this because …" and prompt each party to finish the sentence. When each provides an answer, drill down further by starting a new statement using their previous answer. Repeat this step until you feel you've uncovered the root cause. You can recognize the root cause has been identified when both parties feel settled and satisfied.

When you think you're finished, you can wrap it up by asking, "Is that all?" or "What other reasons cause you to specifically want this thing?" As you build their list of assumptions, push them further by using superlatives. "Is this the *only* thing that will give you what you want?" The purpose of pressing them is to test the reasonability of their assumptions.

You can also follow up with confirmation of what they really are asserting by saying it back to them in different terms. This isn't to trap them but to ensure their logic is completely sound and can be substantiated and verified by them.

Beware! The more you question a person about their assumptions, the more likely you are to meet resistance. Sometimes you encounter reason, and at times, rage. Do not use manipulative tactics such as threats. Tread very carefully here.

This is not the time to be a judge or to interject your opinion. Instead, ask a simple three-word question: "Is that reasonable?"

Listen after asking each of those sincere questions. Don't talk or comment. Just listen. "Silence is one of the hardest arguments to refute."[13]

This reasonability test clarifies the thinking process and sets the brain free from an emotionally hijacked state. It clarifies whether statements are legitimate and well thought out, or if they are based on cognitive dissonance or false narratives.

So, where do we start when trying to test each underlying assumption? The answer is to begin with the most obvious one. If one assumption seems easy to eliminate, begin there. Repeat the steps for each assumption until you can tell that you have uncovered the important, relevant assumptions.

## Consensus Diagram:
### Assumptions

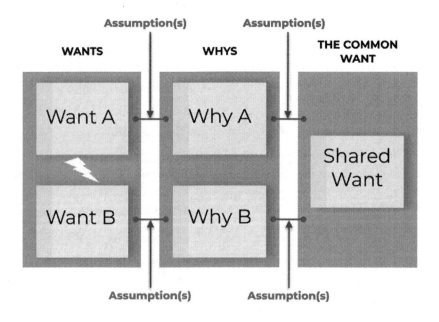

**Case study illustration:** Let's test it out on our animal friends. Reviewing the Consensus Diagram below, which connection appears to be the most unreasonable? Is there a glaring false assumption? Let's begin with the logic line that connects *I love bacon* and *We want peace of mind.*

I turn to the wolf and inquire, "Mr. Wolf, peace of mind comes *because* you love bacon? Are you certain about that?"

"Yes!" he says matter-of-factly.

Taking the superlative approach, I ask, "So you're saying the *only thing* on the face of the earth that would *ever* give you peace of mind is bacon? Is that what you are saying?"

"Well, no—not if you put it like that," he answers, sheepishly.

"Are there other things that would give you peace of mind?"

"Yes."

"Like what?"

"Chicken."

Once that false assumption is exposed (*only bacon offers peace of mind*), I can move to another connecting line—the one between *I want to eat bacon* and *I love bacon*.

"Mr. Wolf, can I ask another question?"

"Why do I feel like I'm being set up here?" he growls.

Tapping a finger on the Consensus Diagram, I respond, "These are your answers, aren't they? I didn't put words into your mouth, did I?"

"No, no, you didn't."

"Okay, so you want to eat bacon *because* you love bacon. Is that right?"

"Yes."

No false assumption found there, so then I ask, "Is that the *only* thing you love to eat?"

"No."

With encouragement, I ask, "Well, what else do you love to eat?"

"Like I said, I like chicken."

Wanting to make the point, I entreat the wolf, "Do you *love* chicken?"

"I guess I do."

Pressing further I reply, "If all you had to eat every day of your life was bacon, would you still love it?"

Pausing, the wolf considers the question. "No, I suppose it would get old after a while."

Patting him gently on the head, I affirm, "Thanks for your candor, Mr. Wolf."

The pigs have a look of relief on their faces. Smiling, I investigate the line between *We want to live* and *We want peace of mind*.

"Does just being alive provide you peace of mind?"

All three of them nod their chinny chin chins simultaneously.

With greater expression, I add, "So if all you did was lie around in your houses, just hanging out, would that give you peace of mind?"

Their eyes dart about as they look at each other. The mason pig clears his throat and remarks, "No, no—we don't like sitting around. We get our satisfaction from building and being industrious. That's what brings us peace of mind!"

## Consensus Diagram Example:
### Assumptions Tested

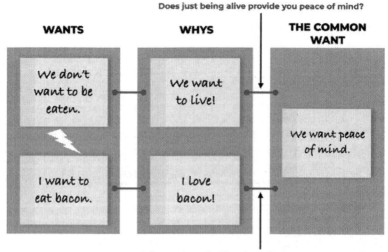

202

## Step 7. Craft a *solution.*

This final step is where you as the mediator may help them craft an agreeable solution that satisfies both parties. While their consideration should be high at this point, their creativity still may need some assistance. With positive emotions engaged, they have an increased ability to come up with new rational solutions.

**What to do:** Ask each party if they have alternative-solution ideas to explore that support both the shared want and the new rationale that emerged from the false assumption tests. If they find it difficult to come up with ideas for a win-win solution, you can make suggestions for their consideration.

**Case study illustration:** Validating the pigs' preferences for being industrious, I ask them a clarifying question.

"Do you build more than just houses?" I inquire.

"Why, yes! We'll build just about anything."

"Would you consider building a chicken restaurant?"

"Yes! We build *and* we cook. You should see the giant cauldron sitting in the fireplace of the brick house right now. Putting that to good use would give us a lot of satisfaction!" they exclaim.

Turning to the wolf, I probe, "Would you eat at their chicken restaurant if they let you?"

"Yes, I would like that very much. That would be far easier than pursuing pigs all day."

"Good deal!" I announce. "Looks like we have a win-win solution."

Both the pigs and the wolf appear truly happy. They shake hooves and paws with some trepidation, but with no sense of compromise.

---

Ideally, a true win-win solution has
no sense of compromise.

---

## The Power of Practice

Teaching and discussing The Consensus Diagram inevitably brings up this question every time: Why don't you provide real-life examples of how this tool solves truly difficult conflicts? Having considered this question and many possible answers and examples, my response is that you just have to try it. Because of the diversity of wants and their associated emotional attachments, there is simply no way to satisfactorily address treacherous conflicts.

Have I addressed some true, hot-button topics? Yes, in live sessions, I have had in-person groups debate many scenarios and difficult topics that would likely raise some eyebrows. And yet, relating them here couldn't ever fully communicate the emotions, perspectives, and considerations that entered those conversations and enabled an outcome of consensus. Your own perspective, wants, and assumptions wouldn't be the same as those in the room who had the discussion. So, for that reason I don't include them here.

Only through the power of experience can you fully grasp the principles and learn the techniques. By practicing the process of using this tool, you will come to understand its efficacy, power, and utility for resolving your own real-life conflicts.

## Connecting the Principles

Success with The Consensus Diagram increases with practice and experience. The more you think about your own assumptions, the better you will become at finding the false ones.

Are you ready for a practice exercise? Perhaps choose one of these:

- Use the Kayla and Alan story to mentally walk through the Consensus Diagram and fill in what you think Kayla and Alan might say. Or, find two friends and have them read the story about Kayla and Alan. Have each of them assume one of the roles and then walk through the steps. Pretend that you have Alan on one side of the locked door and Kayla on the other while you mediate.

- Choose a real conflict or your own personal conflict experience and use it to practice the steps described in the application of The Consensus Diagram. Find out if you can resolve the conflict by identifying the shared want and assumptions then testing the assumptions to identify them as true or false.

NOTE: Some solutions could initiate other problems. For example, in "The Three Little Pigs" story, we might have to start all over and resolve a new conflict between the pigs and the chickens who also want to live in peace. Resolving conflict is more of an art than it is a science.

# Cultivating Harmony and Respect

Truly upright individuals want to build others rather than contending with them or tearing them down. Using The Consensus Diagram can calm tensions and help opposing entities discern the underlying causes of conflict in a more considerate way. The potential of The Consensus Diagram lies in its utility to help expose the false assumptions, expand consideration, and increase harmony as we solve problems together. It is not intended to belittle someone or prove they are wrong; we diminish our own respect and influence when we use it for selfish purposes. Once we master the steps of The Consensus Diagram and practice them in various situations, we can dissect disagreements without having to draw them out on paper. Only when we pick it up and use it will the power of any tool be realized.

CHAPTER 9

# TRANSFORMATION

*"It may be hard for an egg to turn into a
bird; it would be a jolly sight harder for it to
learn to fly while remaining an egg."*

—C.S. Lewis

What do you want? Whatever it is, you can do it! Transformation begins with you. If you want the power that comes from living with consideration, take your newfound awareness and make the change. Identify your wants, then adjust them as necessary. If you want to alter the atmosphere of your family, the organization where you work, or your community, reinvent *your wants* before trying to influence others.

Most humans ultimately want the same things. When we learn to regulate our wants and harmonize them with the people around us, we can make a powerful, positive impact toward those shared desires. We might just obtain what we *all* really want. The concepts in this book form a master plan for change that begins within each individual.

The following three true stories exemplify, respectively, how one person's upright transformation affected their own life, how another's switch changed the lives of people within a business, and how an individual's right-sided thinking helped establish an entire nation!

# Upright Wants Transform Individuals

I conducted an interview with Kristy (name changed), who told me her transformation story and gave permission for me to include it here as she described it to me in an interview.

At the tender age of fourteen, Kristy's parents divorced; her mother remarried, and then the family moved to Alaska where her favorite sport, softball, was nonexistent. Feeling like she had lost everything, Kristy began smoking pot to fill the void. New friends who loved to party helped her overcome feelings of abandonment. Despite the change in lifestyle, she maintained excellent grades. Kristy wasn't dumb; she was just distressed. It seemed to her that everything that she wanted in her young life had crumbled, and she felt unstable.

Shortly after graduation, she married her high school sweetheart, Bill, who also came from her crowd of junkies. Both became addicts by their early twenties. After four years of marriage, Kristy and Bill had a baby boy, but that didn't seem to change the course of their drug-driven lifestyle until consequences blew up. Turning to religion, Kristy sought a different, more peaceful spirit in her life, hoping it would pull her away from her addictions. Bill didn't want anything to do with change. After their second child was born, Kristy and Bill divorced. With the addition of her daughter, Kristy recognized it was more important than ever to escape the drug-addict lifestyle she had foolishly lived. What she really wanted was to be loved and to create an affectionate, safe environment in which she could raise her children.

Kristy eventually found love with another man named Matt. Sadly, it wasn't long before Matt revealed the same addictions and became more abusive than Bill. Daily routines included cocaine and meth. Life became hell again. Authorities shut down Kristy's daycare business when a parent noticed drug paraphernalia in her home. She did everything she could to break free from her miserable life by enrolling in a drug treatment program.

During her time in rehab, she went through a rigorous detox and recovery process. But that wasn't enough. She found herself cheating on her drug tests by having her small daughter supply the urine samples. Kristy remembers her sheer disbelief when she met another woman in the treatment program who was ten years sober. She thought to herself, "There is no way!"

Then she remembered what she really wanted. She wanted real love. She wanted a better life for her kids. She had to find a way to adjust her distance from her addictions. On her own, she sought help from a spiritual advisor. Together, they created a written plan to help her remember what she really wanted. He told her to buy a calendar, and for each day she was clean, to write a "W" for winner. Every day that she succumbed to drugs or alcohol, she was instructed to write "L" for loser. With consideration, she said *okay* to the recommendation, aligning her wants with her upright mentor.

Her first six days were Ls. The seventh was a W. Once she wrote that first W, her competitive nature took over, and she was hooked, but this time, to something positive. Inspired by the dopamine reward of feeling like a winner, Kristy never looked back. Her calendar filled with Ws, which further inspired her to make additional plans for adjusting her distance from anything that would cause an L to appear on her calendar!

After a year of Ws, Kristy found stability. She met a new man named Perry, who was the kindest, cleanest, most loving man she had ever known. He married her for the goodness and purity he saw in her, and he took her children under his wing and loved them like they were his own family.[1]

Kristy did it! Since June 22, 2006, Kristy has had nothing but Ws on her calendar. She achieved what she really wanted: a family filled with peace, love, respect, and honor. She is living proof that long-term change is possible. She now lives these principles and thrives as a powerful, upright woman. She facilitates addiction recovery programs and has been an inspiring example who has helped hundreds of people stuck in upside-down circumstances. Extreme upside-down lives can be made upright when we consistently apply the principles of The Core.

# Upright Wants Transform Organizations

No one *wanted* the COVID-19 pandemic to change their lives, but it did. The infectious virus changed the world in ways no one predicted; there were lots of victims—both in personal respects and in business.

BioSkin, an American company that designs, manufactures, and distributes medical devices, was dramatically affected by the pandemic. By the beginning of April 2020, the United States federal government had declared that all non-essential medical procedures had to be canceled or postponed to prevent the spread of the virus in medical facilities. BioSkin's sales plummeted. Revenue dropped to less than 20 percent of normal, leaving most of the staff without work. After careful consideration and much consternation, the executive team furloughed most of the employees to conserve cash while they continued to work without pay. No one *wanted* this.

At that time, I was president of BioSkin and responsible for the operations of the company. Of course, I didn't *want* the virus to destroy the business I had worked so hard to help improve. At first, I was angry and frustrated by the declining sales and loss of income, both for the company and my personal bank account. Irrational conclusions filled my head as I sat at home, hoping the virus would go away in a week or two.

Then I woke up one morning remembering *The Invisible Four-letter Word* that I had been developing for many years. I declared to the CEO with determination, "I will not be a victim! We are not going to participate in this economic downturn." I knew that I had the power to choose whatever it was I wanted.

Taking a deep breath, I jumped headlong into The Core and resolved, "Okay, we have a virus on our hands. Let's *Adjust Our Distance* and turn this problem around." Armed with an upright attitude, my creativity kicked in, and I jumped on the internet. *If medical providers aren't dispensing medical devices, what do they need instead?* I asked myself. After some quick research and a phone call to a local doctor, I discovered medical facilities needed disposable isolation gowns and N95 face masks.

What we as company really wanted was to help hospitals save lives and keep their employees safe from the virus. Using consideration with renewed resolve, I pulled our staff together and reviewed the raw materials in our inventory. We discovered thousands of yards of polyethylene plastic that could be used to make disposable isolation gowns. I hopped in my truck and drove to the nearby hospital to secure a sample gown.

Back at the plant, this proactive response spread like wildfire. The product designer reverse-engineered the sample, and within hours, the pattern was digitized for the computerized cutting machine. The operator unfurled the materials onto the cutting table, installed the digital file, and produced several samples from the polyethylene material. Wanting to help, another employee volunteered to seam-seal the sleeves. Hours later, I drove to the hospital with a physical prototype for the executive team to evaluate. The design was perfect, and the materials were approved.

Next, I secured an order for 5,000 units, which turned into 15,000, and soon other hospitals from around the country heard about the availability of disposable isolation gowns from BioSkin. Within two weeks, we had tens of thousands of gowns on order. Every employee was called back to work, and an additional 30 people were hired to manufacture gowns around the clock.

Combining an upright attitude with proactivity not only helped rescue the company, but it also inspired BioSkin's CEO, Tanner Cropper. After hearing my proclamation that we were not going to participate in the downturn, Tanner acted on an insight that the world was going to need cloth masks to supplement the N95 mask market that was being overwhelmed by massive demand. His proactive approach turned into a new multimillion-dollar product category for BioSkin.

Working together, our right-sided approach saved our business and our personal financial situations, bolstered the well-being of others, and most importantly, helped protect the lives of healthcare workers who needed masks and gowns, which were quickly becoming scarce. By changing my own initial upside-down response to an upright approach, I became a powerful problem solver who inspired others and affected many lives in positive ways.

## Upright Wants Transform the World

By December of 1776, the American Revolutionary War appeared bleak for the exhausted American patriots. The combined British and German Hessian forces were proving impenetrable, but General George Washington refused to be beaten. On Christmas day, with the weather turning perilous, Washington wrote and rewrote the same message on tiny sheets of paper: "Victory or Death." That message represented what the adamant General Washington wanted! Washington also sent an urgent note to General John Cadwalader declaring, "I am determined, as the night is favorable, to cross the river and make an attack on Trenton in the morning."[2]

Simultaneously, across the Delaware river, Colonel Johann Gottlieb Rall occupied himself in a small house in the village of Trenton. His Hessian army had seized the deserted town and made themselves at home.

Junior officers described Rall as lazy and apathetic, taking extreme pleasure in drinking and playing cards.

A severe northeaster storm arose that was reported to blow like a hurricane. Freezing temperatures choked the Delaware River with chunks of ice. Washington stood undaunted in his desires, while Rall was ready for another round of cards in his cozy cottage. As Washington led his exhausted and freezing band of rebels across the wintry waters, Rall received a message from an unnamed loyalist, warning him of the impending attack. Not wanting to be troubled during his game of cards and unable to read English, Rall casually dismissed the note, stuffing it into his pocket. After consuming even more alcohol, the colonel retired to his quarters.

At roughly 8:00 p.m. on December 26th, General Washington's army attacked Trenton. The Patriots moved so swiftly into the village that the Hessians were wildly confused. Washington's men engaged in house-to-house fighting until the Hessians opted for retreat. Colonel Rall, rousted from his drunken slumber, was quickly thrust into the wintry storm. His own men fell like sleet around him, and then he was hit and dropped from his horse with a mortal wound.

This was the turning point in the American Revolutionary War. On a tiny note, Washington had written what he wanted, what he *really* wanted. His mental and physical determination bolstered himself and his troops. Washington's upright leadership united his men, energizing them with the desire to press on to victory—even in the harshest of storms.

On the other hand, Rall had wanted only what *he* wanted. His self-serving game of cards and a few drinks revealed his lack of consideration. Not *wanting* to read the warning note that was handed to him in a moment of peril changed the course of history![3]

# The Secret to Getting What You Really Want

Now that you know the human tendencies surrounding the invisible four-letter word, you can improve the relationships with those around you, reduce conflicts in your life, and enjoy achieving more of what you really want. Embracing these principles helps achieve what you really want by choosing what is best over what you might naturally want right now. You can resolve individual problems between a parent and a child, problems in a business between managers and employees, family difficulties between husbands and wives—and you can dissolve personal, inner conflict. If everyone could learn to apply upright responses to their wants, the positive influence on humanity could be monumental!

In summary, wants act as an invisible force, luring us from one moment to the next and driving even our smallest decisions. Becoming aware of the Six Dimensions of Desire enables us to analyze the complex facets of our wants, how they change the nature of our choices, and how they affect others. The Choice Spectrum illustrates the relationship between selflessness and love or selfishness and hatred and their influence on the decisions we make. Our free will allows us to choose the location, direction, and velocity of our wants on the Choice Spectrum.

Everyone vacillates between feeling upside down or right side up. Both upside-down and upright reactions come from what we want. When we don't get what we want, unchecked negative emotions can lead to irrational conclusions as our brain is hijacked, often tricking it into making false assumptions. Mental misgivings may then re-route a reactive response toward a powerless position. This upside-down chain of events can destabilize us like an inverted pyramid in the Egyptian desert sand.

Practicing the regulation of our wants produces lifelong benefits. When we have moments of feeling upside down, the four conventions of The Core can help transform our upside-down responses to a more powerful, upright mindset. When we *Begin with Consideration*, our opportunities multiply. *Just Say Okay* cancels the effects of negative emotions and suspends the conflict, allowing us to rationally consider other perspectives. *Adjust Your Distance* means we conscientiously get closer to things we want while getting away from things we don't want. *Remembering What You Really Want* reminds us to subordinate our short-term decisions to our long-term goals and most valuable desires.

As we regulate our wants and harmonize them with other people and their wants, we experience positive emotions and enhance our rational thinking and creativity. We see things more clearly, even when encountering situations that we don't really want. These right-sided habits also empower us to be more proactive and expand our opportunities. With this growth mindset, we can be powerful allies who are fair, thoughtful, and honorable.

Beyond The Core, The Consensus Diagram provides a process for overcoming even the most challenging disagreements. Most conflicts arise from false expectations or erroneous assumptions. Exposing and correcting those fallacies help resolve contention and reveal new solutions for peace.

## What Do You Really Want?

It all comes down to this: What you want is ultimately your decision. The availability of so many different wants in modern society requires you to make choices, but each individual desire at some point directly or indirectly impacts other people. This interdependent relationship between individuals' wants and the complex nature of wants means that subsequent choices do not and cannot exist in a vacuum. Harmony inside yourself and with other people (and therefore the degree to which you flourish) increases as you *recognize* then *regulate* the natural struggle that exists between conflicting wants in their various forms, the diverse wants of others, and your responses to those wants.

This book declares the invisible four-letter word to be both a friend and an enemy—because sometimes your wants save you, but other times they condemn you. What you want can foster love or may provoke hate. Those desires promote harmony or instigate discord. Your wants determine if you blossom like a rose or become prickly like a cactus. They can throw you into the brig of bondage or liberate you from dependence. The paradox of wants is that while you own your wants, they also can own you. Wants represent both a burden and a blessing in the opportunity to express your free will because your response to your wants either elevates you with honor or douses you with disdain. Each of these dichotomous phrases represents a fork in the road where you must choose what *you really want*. The good news is that old wants can always be replaced by better wants. Every decision you make contributes to your potential power and influence.

So, what do you *really* want? This is your call to action. The formerly invisible four-letter word stands prominently before you.

Mahatma Gandhi declared, "If we could change ourselves, the tendencies in the world would also change. As a man changes his own nature, so does the attitude of the world change towards him. This is the divine mystery supreme. A wonderful thing it is and the source of our happiness. We need not wait to see what others do."[4]

Now, take an upright approach to life by recognizing and regulating your wants so you can get what you *really* WANT!

# EPILOGUE

Michael called me out of the blue one day. It had been six years since we had last seen each other. Shocked and surprised to hear from him, I eagerly asked, "How are you doing?"

"I'm doing great!" he replied with certitude. "Been sober for several years now, and I'm not looking back."

"That's fantastic, Michael! What was the key?" I asked.

"Staying right sided. I try to remember what I really want in life," he replied. "Being around my boys regularly and steadily climbing out of financial ruin has been very fulfilling. I want to be the best dad I can to my boys, and I want stability. I want to be a trusted and productive member of society."

"I'm proud of you," I affirmed. "How does it feel?"

"It feels awesome!" he responded. "But it's not easy. There's always the temptation to slide back into what I want now."

"How do you stay away from those temptations?" I inquired.

"I give all my energy to The Core. It takes some serious focus and a whole lot of consideration to want what others want. But, if I can do it, anyone can do it—if they *want* to," he emphasized.

"You've done a great thing with your life, Michael," I replied.

"Thanks for your help, love, and especially, for believing in me."

# ACKNOWLEDGEMENTS

First and foremost, none of this would have been possible were it not for my dear friend, Michael. The humble declaration that he was being crushed by an upside-down pyramid started the whole process of discovery. Together, we identified the cause-and-effect relationships of the invisible four-letter word. Thank you, Michael! Your painful declaration is changing lives.

To my family, who has been the primary laboratory for the whole book: There is no better place to experiment with the invisible four-letter word than within the walls of our own home. That is where we discover what we really, really want. All my children, Danielle, Bryce, Sheralyn, Tanner, Madeline, and Janelle offered constant encouragement to complete this project.

My wife Wendy scoured the drafts several times. She was honest, forthright, and fantastic with her comments. I told her from the beginning that what I really wanted was a book that made a powerful impact in the world. She hacked and slashed the manuscript like a pirate taking no prisoners. Her bravery and honesty were awesome!

Special thanks to Joshua Cooke who helped identify some of the psychological underpinnings at the beginning of the book's development. Brock Bumgarner furnished most of the studies and research connections that support the underlying principles of *The Invisible Four-letter Word*. Brock's contribution took this project to the next level.

Lisa Burt, the content editor, provided masterful wordsmithing. Questioning every part of the book, she put it through a high-pressure, reasonability test. She tinkered with every element of the book to ensure it had proper meaning, purpose, and efficacy. Her attention to detail is second to none.

Along the way, there were many cheerleaders, editors, contributors, and people who helped with this work and pressed for their personal copies at all stages of development: Brian and Candace Green, Brigham Rupp, Dr. Ted Bennion, Scott Bybee, Sadie Burt, Julie Golding, Marvin Jessee, Kristine Case, Tim Pritchett, Valerie Blazer, Ken and Sally Hollinzer, Steve Rice, Anna Kaegi, Kelly Anderson, Mary Anne Cropper, Tanner Cropper, Chalyse Gillespie, and many others. Thank you to all who added to and cheered on this work. Every one of you helped me remember what I really wanted.

Isaac Newton penned these insightful words in a letter to his rival Robert Hooke, "If I have seen further, it is by standing on the shoulders of Giants."[1]

There are three specific giants who have influenced this work beyond the feeble limits of words on paper. First, Dr. Eliyahu M. Goldratt who inspires me to focus on that which matters most. Second, King Benjamin, of the Nephite nation who first described the upside-down pyramid metaphor in his "natural man" speech.[2] Finally, and most importantly, Jesus, the Son of God, whose life work was devoted to "doing the will (want) of his Father." Jesus is, and ever will be, the greatest upright example to walk this earth!

# ADDITIONAL RESOURCES

For additional resources, training materials, and online tools about *The Invisible Four-letter Word*, visit invisiblefourletterword.com.

To inquire about a possible speaking engagement or for specialized training, visit emiment.com, email us at info@emiment.com, or call us at 309-emiment (309-364-6368).

# Notes

## CHAPTER 2 — CONFLICT

1. Joseph Grenny, Kerry Patterson, David Maxfield, Ron McMillan, and Al Switzler, *Influencer: The New Science of Leading Change*, 2nd ed. (US: McGraw-Hill, 2013).
2. Scott Frankowski, Amber K. Lupo, Brandt A. Smith, Mosi Dane'El, Corin Ramos, and Osvaldo F. Morera, "Developing and testing a scale to measure need for drama." *Personality and Individual Differences* 89 (2016): 192-201.
3. William Ellery Channing, quoted on Brainyquote (website), www.brainyquote.com/quotes/william_ellery_channing_132566.
4. Philip H. Knight, *Shoe Dog: A Memoir by the Creator of Nike*. (New York: Scribner, 2016).

## CHAPTER 3 — THE NATURE OF WANT

1. Joel Hoomans, "35,000 Decisions: The Great Choices of Strategic Leaders," *The Leading Edge* (2015). https://go.roberts.edu/leadingedge/the-great-choices-of-strategic-leaders.
2. A.H. Maslow, "A theory of human motivation," *Psychological Review*, 50 (1943): 370-96.
3. W. Crain, Theories of Development: Concepts and Applications, 5th ed. (2005).
4. Michael Tomasello and Hannes Rakoczy, "What makes human cognition unique? From individual to shared to collective intentionality," *Mind & language* 18, no. 2 (2003): 121-147.
5. Saul McLeod, "Freewill vs Determinism in Psychology," *Freewill and Determinism, Simply Psychology,* Olivia Guy-Evans, reviewer (website), Simply Scholar, Ltd., (2019, updated October 10, 2023), www.simplypsychology.org/freewill-determinism.html.
6. Roy F. Baumeister, The Cultural Animal: Human Nature, Meaning, and Social Life (Oxford University Press, 2005).
7. Denis G. Arnold, "Hume on the Moral Difference between Humans and other Animals," *History of Philosophy Quarterly* 12, no. 3 (1995): 303-316.

8. Stephanie Glen, "Normal Distributions (Bell Curve): Definition, Word Problems," From StatisticsHowTo.com: Elementary Statistics for the rest of us! (website), https://www.statisticshowto.com/probability-and-statistics/normal-distributions/.

9. Alex Kendrick and Stephen Kendrick, *Love Dare* (Nashville: B&H Publishing Group 2014).

10. Matthew 6:10 (KJV).

11. John 15:13 (KJV).

12. Diana Ross, "Do You Know Where You're Going To?" *Touch Me in the Morning,* (Motown Records, 1973).

## CHAPTER 4 — THE UPSIDE-DOWN PYRAMID

1. Stephen E. Newstead, Paul Pollard, Jonathan St. BT Evans, and Julie L. Allen, "The source of belief bias effects in syllogistic reasoning," *Cognition* 45, no. 3 (1992): 257-284.

2. Kent C. Berridge, "Wanting and liking: Observations from the neuroscience and psychology laboratory," *Inquiry* 52, no. 4 (2009): 378-398.

3. Exodus 20:17 (KJV).

4. "Lexicon: Strong's H2530--ḥāmaḏ," Blue Letter Bible (website), Blue Letter Bible Institute, www.blueletterbible.org/lexicon/h2530/kjv/wlc/0-1/.

5. Ibid.

6. 1 Corinthians 12:31 (KJV).

7. Eva Pool, Tobias Brosch, Sylvain Delplanque, and David Sander, "Stress increases cue-triggered 'wanting' for sweet reward in humans," *Journal of Experimental Psychology: Animal Learning and Cognition* 41, no. 2 (2015): 128.

8. D. Augustine GJ. Purves, D. Fitzpatrick, et al., "The Interplay of Emotion and Reason," *Neuroscience*, 2nd ed. (Sunderland, MA: Sinauer Associates, 2001).

9. Walter Mischel, *The Marshmallow Test: Why Self-control is the Engine of Success*, reprint ed. (New York: Little, Brown, 2015).

10. Liz Mineo, "Good genes are nice, but joy is better," *The Harvard Gazette* 11 (2017).

11. Jane Their, "Slack's CEO pinpoints the problem with the return to office: 'People don't want to be told what to do,'" *Fortune Magazine* (October 21, 2022).

12. Lauren A. Leotti, et al, "Born to choose: the origins and value of the need for control," *Trends in Cognitive Sciences* vol. 14, no. 10 (2010): 457-63.

13. C. S. Carver, "Self-awareness," in M. R. Leary and J. P. Tangney, *Handbook of Self and Identity* (New York: Guilford, 2003): 179-196.

14. Lawrence James Cookson, "Differences between feelings, emotions and desires in terms of interactive quality," *Advances in Social Sciences Research Journal* 2, no. 7 (2015).

15. Marco Leyton, "The neurobiology of desire: Dopamine and the regulation of mood and motivational states in humans," M. L. Kringelbach and K. C. Berridge, eds., *Pleasures of the Brain* (Oxford University Press, 2010): 222–243.

16. Elena Baixauli Gallego, "Happiness: role of dopamine and serotonin on mood and negative emotions," *Emergency Medicine* (Los Angeles), vol. 6, no. 2 (2017): 33-51.

17. Robert James R. Blair, "Considering anger from a cognitive neuroscience perspective," Wiley Interdisciplinary Reviews: *Cognitive Science* 3, no. 1 (2012): 65-74.

18. "Upset" definition, Dictionary.com (website), Dictionary.com, LLC, https://www.dictionary.com/browse/upset.

19. Robert James R. Blair, *Cognitive Science,* 65-74.

20. Seneca, "Anger," *A Dictionary of Thoughts,* edited by Tryon Edwards (Cassell Publishing Company 1891): 21.

21. D. Purves, GJ Augustine, D. Fitzpatrick, et al., eds., "The Interplay of Emotion and Reason," *Neuroscience*, 2nd ed. (Sunderland, MA: Sinauer Associates, 2001).

22. Antonio R. Damásio, "Emotion and the Human Brain," *Annals of the New York Academy of Sciences* 935, no. 1 (2001): 101-106.

23. Ahmad Alipour, et al., "Emotional Intelligence and Prefrontal Cortex: a Comparative Study Based on Wisconsin Card Sorting Test (WCST)," *Iranian journal of Psychiatry and Behavioral Sciences* vol. 5, no 2 (2011): 114-9.

24. Arlin Cuncic, "Amygdala Hijack and the Fight or Flight Response," Verywellmind (website), Dotdash Media, Inc., (updated June 22, 2021), https://www.verywellmind.com/what-happens-during-an-amygdala-hijack-4165944.

25. Gloria Willcox, "The Feeling Wheel: A Tool for Expanding Awareness of Emotions and Increasing Spontaneity and Intimacy," *Transactional Analysis Journal* 12, no. 4 (October 1982): 274–76.

26. Ibid.

27. Marion D. Hanks, "Forgiveness: The Ultimate Form of Love," *Ensign Magazine,* January 1974.

28. Alice MacLachlan, "Unreasonable resentments," *Journal of Social Philosophy* 41, no. 4 (2010).

29. R.D. Enright and R. Fitzgibbons, *Forgiveness Therapy* (Washington, DC: APA Books, 2014).

30. Benedetto De Martino, et al., "Frames, biases, and rational decision-making in the human brain," *Science* vol. 313, 5787 (2006): 684-7.

31. Daniel Goleman, *Emotional Intelligence: Why It Can Matter More Than IQ*, 10th Anniversary ed. (Random House Publishing Group, September 27, 2005).

32. Barbara A. Weiner, "Not guilty by reason of insanity: A sane approach," *Chicago-Kent Law Review* 56, no. 4 (1980): 1057.

33. Stuart Wolpert, "Putting feelings into words produces therapeutic effects in the brain; UCLA neuroimaging study supports ancient Buddhist teachings," *UCLA Newsroom* 21 (2007): 132-138.

34. Matthew 5:25 (KJV).

35. A. Megías, M.J. Gutiérrez-Cobo, and R. Gómez-Leal, et al., "Performance on emotional tasks engaging cognitive control depends on emotional intelligence abilities: an ERP study." *Scientific Reports* 7, 16446 (2017).

36. Thomas Curran, Andrew P. Hill, Paul R. Appleton, Robert J. Vallerand, and Martyn Standage, "The psychology of passion: A meta-analytical review of a decade of research on intrapersonal outcomes," *Motivation and Emotion* 39 (2015): 631-655.

37. Robert J. Vallerand, *The Psychology of Passion: A Dualistic Model*, Oxford Scholarship Online (August 2015).

38. Publius Syrus, "Anger," In *A Dictionary of Thoughts,* Tryon Edwards, ed. (Cassell Publishing Company, 1891): 21.

39. "Erroneous"definition, Dictionary.com (website), Dictionary.com, LLC, www.dictionary.com/browse/erroneous.

40. Proverbs 18:13 (KJV).

41. Cameron Martel, Gordon Pennycook, and David G. Rand, "Reliance on emotion promotes belief in fake news," *Cognitive Research: Principles and Implications* vol. 5, art. 47 (7 Oct. 2020): 1-20.

42. Drew Westen, Pavel S. Blagov, Keith Harenski, Clint Kilts, and Stephan Hamann, "Neural bases of motivated reasoning: An fMRI study of emotional constraints on partisan political judgment in the 2004 US presidential election," *Journal of Cognitive Neuroscience* 18, no. 11 (2006): 1947-1958.

43. Martel, et al., *Cognitive Research: Principles and Implications*, 1-20.

44. Katia M. Harlé, Pradeep Shenoy, and Martin P. Paulus, "The influence of emotions on cognitive control: feelings and beliefs—where do they meet?," *Frontiers in Human Neuroscience* 7 (2013): 508.

45. "What is a self-schema?" from 3-S Theoretical Foundation, Yale School of Medicine (website), archived from the original on February 4, 2013, retrieved 5 May 2013, https://medicine.yale.edu/spiritualselfschema/about/foundation/.

46. E. Harmon-Jones, "Cognitive Dissonance Theory," *Encyclopedia of Human Behavior,* 2nd ed. (2012).

47. Jay Weaver, "American Airlines mechanic sentenced to three years for tampering with plane in Miami," *Miami Herald,* March 4, 2020, https://www.miamiherald.com/news/local/article240876846.html.

48. Eric Jaffe, "The complicated psychology of revenge," *APS Observer* 24, (2011).

49. Chris Tompkins and Josh Kear, "Before He Cheats," Performed by Carrie Underwood on her debut album, *Some Hearts* (Universal Music Group, 2005).

50. Kevin M. Carlsmith, Timothy D. Wilson, and Daniel T. Gilbert.,"The paradoxical consequences of revenge." *Journal of Personality and Social Psychology* 95, no. 6 (2008): 1316.

51. Julia C. Babcock, Charles E. Green, Sarah A. Webb, and Timothy P. Yerington, "Psychophysiological profiles of batterers: autonomic emotional reactivity as it predicts the antisocial spectrum of behavior among intimate partner abusers," *Journal of Abnormal Psychology* 114, no. 3 (2005): 444.

52. Benjamin G. Shapero, Amy Farabaugh, Olga Terechina, Stephanie DeCross, Joey C. Cheung, Maurizio Fava, and Daphne J. Holt, "Understanding the effects of emotional reactivity on depression and suicidal thoughts and behaviors: Moderating effects of childhood adversity and resilience," *Journal of Affective Disorders* 245 (2019): 419-427.

53. Astrid Schüutz, "It was your fault! Self-serving biases in autobiographical accounts of conflicts in married couples," *Journal of Social and Personal Relationships* 16, no. 2 (1999): 193-208.

54. Herman Melville, "Bartleby, the Scrivener: A Story of Wall Street" (a short story by the American writer, first serialized anonymously in two parts in the November and December 1853 issues of *Putnam's Magazine* and reprinted with minor textual alterations in Melville's *The Piazza Tales* in 1856).

55. "Edward and Elaine Brown," Wikipedia, The Free Encyclopedia (website), https://en.wikipedia.org/wiki/Edward_and_Elaine_Brown.

56. Julia F. Christensen, Steven Di Costa, Brianna Beck, and Patrick Haggard, "I just lost it! Fear and anger reduce the sense of agency: a study using intentional binding," *Experimental Brain Research* 237 (2019): 1205-1212.

57. Dengfeng Wang and Norman H. Anderson, "Excuse-making and blaming as a function of internal—external locus of control," *European Journal of Social Psychology* 24, no. 2 (1994): 295-302.

58. Gabriel Lopez-Garrido, "Locus of Control," Simply Psychology (website), Sept. 13, 2020, Saul Mcleod, reviewer, Simply Scholar, Ltd. (updated August 24, 2023), https://www.simplypsychology.org/locus-of-control.html.

**CHAPTER 5 — HARMONY**

1. Michael N. Cline, from his personal journal dated January 2018.
2. Jordan B. Peterson, "Lecture: Biblical Series I: Introduction to the Idea of God," from the lecture series *The Psychological Significance of the Biblical Stories: Genesis,* YouTube (website), May 20, 2017, https://youtu.be/f-wWBGo6a2w at time mark 00:38:20.
3. Albert Von Tilzer, "Take Me Out to the Ball Game," 1908, In *Baseball's Greatest Hits: The Best Music from America's Game*, John Smith, ed. (Chicago: Music Publishing Company, 2010): 45-47.
4. Larissa Conradt and Timothy J. Roper, "Democracy in animals: the evolution of shared group decisions," *Proceedings of the Royal Society* B: Biological Sciences 274, no. 1623 (2007): 2317-2326.

**CHAPTER 6 — THE UPRIGHT PYRAMID**

1. Seneca, "Wants," *A Dictionary of Thoughts,* Tyron Edwards, ed. (Cassell Publishing Company, 1891): 611.
2. D.G. Hewitt, "10 of the Most Heroic Acts of Self-Sacrifice in History," History Collection (website), https://historycollection.com/10-of-the-most-heroic-acts-of-self-sacrifice-in-history/3/.
3. "Kidney Donation: Dylan's Story," John Hopkins Medicine (website), John Hopkins University, original source (no longer available), https://www.hopkinsmedicine.org/transplant/patient_information/patient_%20stories/kidney-donation-dylan-story.html; updated story can be found at https://www.hopkinsmedicine.org/health/treatment-tests-and-therapies/kidney-transplant/patient-story-kidney-donation-dylan.
4. Dr. Seuss, *Oh, the Places You'll Go!* (Random House, 1990).
5. Socrates, found in Tyron Edwards, ed., *The New Dictionary of Thoughts,* (Britkin Publishing Company, 1927): 688.
6. Emily S. Taylor Poppe, "Surprised by the Inevitable: A National Survey of Estate Planning Utilization," *UC Davis Law Review* 53 (2019): 2511.
7. Luke 6:31 (NIV).

8.  Sandra L. Murray, John G. Holmes, and Dale W. Griffin, "The benefits of positive illusions: Idealization and the construction of satisfaction in close relationships," *Journal of Personality and Social Psychology*, vol. 70 (Jan 1996): 79-98.

9.  Randi Fredricks, "Four Behaviors That Predict Divorce," Dr. Randi Fredricks, PhD (website), September 14, 2015, http://drrandifredricks.com/four-behaviors-that-predict-divorce/.

10. W. Bradford Wilcox and Jeffrey Dew, "The social and cultural predictors of generosity in marriage: Gender egalitarianism, religiosity, and familism," *Journal of Family Issues* 37, no. 1 (2016): 97-118.

11. Jennifer Crocker, Amy Canevello, and Ashley A. Brown, "Social motivation: Costs and benefits of selfishness and otherishness," *Annual Review of Psychology* 68, no. 1 (2017): 299-325.

12. Satinder Dhiman, *Holistic Leadership: A New Paradigm for Today's Leaders*, 1st ed. (Palgrave Macmillan, January 12, 2017): 220.

13. Elizabeth W. Dunn, Lara B. Aknin, and Michael I. Norton, "Spending money on others promotes happiness," *Science* 319, no. 5870 (2008): 1687-1688.

14. Tristen K. Inagaki, Kate E. Byrne Haltom, Shosuke Suzuki, Ivana Jevtic, Erica Hornstein, Julienne E. Bower, and Naomi I. Eisenberger, "The neurobiology of giving versus receiving support: the role of stress-related and social reward-related neural activity," *Psychosomatic Medicine* 78, no. 4 (2016): 443.

15. Sören Krach, Frieder M. Paulus, Maren Bodden, and Tilo Kircher, "The rewarding nature of social interactions," *Frontiers in Behavioral Neuroscience* 4 (2010): 22.

16. Krishna G. Seshadri, "The Neuroendocrinology of Love." *Indian Journal of Endocrinology and Metabolism* 20, no. 4 (2016): 558.

17. Barry L. Jacobs and Efrain C. Azmitia, "Structure and function of the brain serotonin system," *Physiological Reviews* 72, no. 1 (1992): 165-229.

18. Hai-Peng Yang, Liwei Wang, Liqun Han, and Stephani C. Wang, "Nonsocial functions of hypothalamic oxytocin," *International Scholarly Research Notices* (2013).

19. Tom Scheve, "Is there a link between exercise and happiness?," HowStuffWorks (website), 22 June 2009, https://science.howstuffworks.com/life/exercise-happiness.htm.

20. Terri Yablonsky Stat, "Be generous: It's a simple way to stay healthier," *Chicago Tribune*, Aug 06, 2015.

21. Claus Wedekind and Victoria A. Braithwaite, "The long-term benefits of human generosity in indirect reciprocity," *Current Biology* 12, no. 12 (2002): 1012-1015.

22. Nadine Jung, Christina Wranke, Kai Hamburger, and Markus Knauff, "How emotions affect logical reasoning: evidence from experiments with mood-manipulated

participants, spider phobics, and people with exam anxiety," *Frontiers in Psychology* 5 (2014): 570.

23. Gloria Willcox, "The Feeling Wheel: A Tool for Expanding Awareness of Emotions and Increasing Spontaneity and Intimacy," *Transactional Analysis Journal* 12, no. 4 (October 1982): 274–76.

24. Christina N. Armenta, Megan M. Fritz, and Sonja Lyubomirsky, "Functions of positive emotions: Gratitude as a motivator of self-improvement and positive change," *Emotion Review* 9, no. 3 (2017): 183-190.

25. Veruska Santos, Flavia Paes, Valeska Pereira, Oscar Arias-Carrión, Adriana Cardoso Silva, Mauro Giovanni Carta, Antonio Egidio Nardi, and Sergio Machado, "The role of positive emotion and contributions of positive psychology in depression treatment: systematic review," *Clinical Practice and Epidemiology in Mental Health* (2013).

26. Peter Salovey and John D. Mayer, "Emotional Intelligence," *Imagination, Cognition and Personality* 9, no. 3 (March 1990): 185–211.

27. Edward Neukrug, *Counseling Theory and Practice,* 2nd ed., (Cognella Academic Publishing, 2017).

28. George Lucas, *Star Wars, Episode III: Revenge of the Sith,* Lucasfilm, Ltd. (2005).

29. Jason Collins, "Rationalizing the 'Irrational'," *Behavioral Scientist* (August 2017).

30. Jim Albert, "The Vanishing 300 Batting Average," *Exploring Baseball Data with R* (blog), https://baseballwithr.wordpress.com/2018/12/24/the-vanishing-300-batting-average/#:~:text=300%20hitters.,hitters%20in%20the%202018%20season.

31. Madoka Kumashiro, Caryl E. Rusbult, and Eli J. Finkel, "Navigating personal and relational concerns: The quest for equilibrium," *Journal of Personality and Social Psychology* 95, no. 1 (2008): 94.

32. Francesca Righetti and Emily Impett, "Sacrifice in close relationships: Motives, emotions, and relationship outcomes," *Social and Personality Psychology Compass* 11, no. 10 (2017): e12342.

33. Richard Whately, "Selfishness," in Tryon Edwards, ed., *A Dictionary of Thoughts* (1891): 515.

34. Susana Claro, David Paunesku, and Carol S. Dweck, "Growth mindset tempers the effects of poverty on academic achievement," *Proceedings of the National Academy of Sciences* 113, no. 31 (2016): 8664-8668.

35. "Dr. Dweck's research into growth mindset changed education forever," from the "Decades of Scientific Research that Started a Growth Mindset Revolution" page, Mindsetworks (website), Mindset Works, Inc., https://www.mindsetworks.com/Science/Default.

36. Mark D. Seery, E. Alison Holman, and Roxane Cohen Silver, "Whatever does not kill us: cumulative lifetime adversity, vulnerability, and resilience," *Journal of Personality and Social Psychology* 99, no. 6 (2010): 1025.

37. Alyssa Croft, Elizabeth W. Dunn, and Jordi Quoidbach, "From tribulations to appreciation: Experiencing adversity in the past predicts greater savoring in the present," *Social Psychological and Personality Science* 5, no. 5 (2014): 511-516.

38. Martin F. Hunt, Jr. and Gerald R. Miller, "Open-and closed-mindedness, belief-discrepant communication behavior, and tolerance for cognitive inconsistency," *Journal of Personality and Social Psychology* 8, no. 1 p1 (1968): 35.

39. Anna Antinori, Olivia L. Carter, and Luke D. Smillie, "Seeing it both ways: Openness to experience and binocular rivalry suppression," *Journal of Research in Personality* 68 (2017): 15-22.

40. Holly G. Prigerson and Paul K. Maciejewski, "Grief and acceptance as opposite sides of the same coin: setting a research agenda to study peaceful acceptance of loss," *The British Journal of Psychiatry* 193, no. 6 (2008): 435-437.

41. Stephen R. Covey, *The Seven Habits of Highly Effective People: Restoring the Character Ethic.* (New York: Simon and Schuster, 1989).

42. Michael McCullough, *Beyond Revenge: The Evolution of the Forgiveness Instinct,* (San Francisco: Jossey-Bass, A Wiley Imprint, 2008).

43. E.C. Martins and F. Terblanche, "Building organizational culture that stimulates creativity and innovation," *European Journal of Innovation Management*, vol 6, no. 1 (2003): 64-74.

44. Peter Economy, "This Study of 300,000 Leaders Revealed the Top 10 Traits for Success," *Inc. Magazine*, Mar. 30, 2018.

45. Leading Effectively Staff, "The 10 Characteristics of a Good Leader," Center for Creative Leadership (website), January 24, 2023, https://www.ccl.org/articles/leading-effectively-articles/characteristics-good-leader.

46. Kelly M. Willenberg, "Attributes of Successful Leaders in Research," *Research Management Review* 20, no. 1 (2014): 1-4.

47. Dale Carnegie, *How to Win Friends and Influence People,* updated ed. (New York: Simon & Schuster, 2022).

48. Shelley Thompkins, "Emotional Intelligence and Leadership Effectiveness: Bringing Out the Best," Center for Creative Leadership (website), https://www.ccl.org/articles/leading-effectively-articles/emotional-intelligence-and-leadership-effectiveness/.

49. Aon Hewitt Study, "People Fuel Growth; How High Growth Companies Leverage Talent," Aon Inc. (2016).

50. Ludwig-Maximilians-Universität München, "Developmental psychology: One good turn deserves another," ScienceDaily (website), September 18, 2019, www.sciencedaily.com/releases/2019/09/190918105645.htm.

51. Albert Payson Terhune, *The Story of Damon and Pythias*, (Grosset & Dunlap, 1915).


**CHAPTER 7 — CHANGING DIRECTION**

1. Stephen R. Covey, *The 7 Habits of Highly Effective People*, 4th ed. (New York: Simon & Schuster, 2020).

2. Sterling W. Ellsworth, *How I Got This Way and What to Do About It*. (Luminare Press, 2021): 84-86.

3. Mark R. Leary, Eleanor B. Tate, Claire E. Adams, Ashley Batts Allen, and Jessica Hancock, "Self-compassion and reactions to unpleasant self-relevant events: the implications of treating oneself kindly," *Journal of Personality and Social Psychology* 92, no. 5 (2007): 887.

4. Yale-NUS College, "A growth mindset of interest can spark innovative thinking," ScienceDaily (website), November 25, 2020, www.sciencedaily.com/releases/2020/11/201125100305.htm.

5. Atin Basuchoudhary, Vahan Simoyan, and Raja Mazumder, "The Evolution of Cooperation: How Patience Matters," available at SSRN 2162149 (2013).

6. Atin Basuchoudhary, Troy Siemers, and Samuel Allen, "Civilization and the evolution of short-sighted agents," available at SSRN 1318367 (2008).

7. Jeffrey D. Ford and Laurie W. Ford, "Decoding Resistance to Change," *Harvard Business Review*, April 2009.

8. Ibid.

9. Olga M. Klimecki, "The role of empathy and compassion in conflict resolution," *Emotion Review* 11, no. 4 (2019): 310-325.

10. "OK" definition, Dictionary.com (website), Dictionary.com, LLC, https://www.dictionary.com/browse/ok.

11. Jordan B. Peterson, *12 Rules for Life* (Random House Canada, 2018): 60.

12. Brett Q. Ford, Phoebe Lam, Oliver P. John, and Iris B. Mauss, "The psychological health benefits of accepting negative emotions and thoughts: Laboratory, diary, and longitudinal evidence," *Journal of Personality and Social Psychology* 115, no. 6 (2018): 1075.

13. Matthew 5:25 (KJV).

14. Sonsoles Valdivia-Salas, José Martín-Albo, Araceli Cruz, Víctor J. Villanueva-Blasco, and Teresa I. Jiménez, "Psychological Flexibility with Prejudices Increases Empathy and Decreases Distress Among Adolescents: A Spanish Validation of the Acceptance and Action Questionnaire–Stigma," *Frontiers in Psychology* 11 (2021): 3911.
15. Jeff Erickson, via Associated Press (untitled photo), November 12, 2016, "Last Stand of Two Bull Moose Encased in Ice," *The Spokesman-Review*, November 29, 2016, https://www.spokesman.com/blogs/outdoors/2016/nov/29/last-stand-bull-moose-encased-ice.
16. Brian Clark Howard, "Two Bull Moose Found Frozen in Mortal Combat," *National Geographic*, Nov. 18, 2016.
17. Jonathan W. Kanter, E. Baruch, and Scott T. Gaynor, "Acceptance and commitment therapy and behavioral activation for the treatment of depression: Description and comparison," *The Behavior Analyst* 29, no. 2 (2006): 161-185.
18. Steven C. Hayes and Heather Pierson, "Acceptance and commitment therapy," *Encyclopedia of Cognitive Behavior Therapy* (2005): 1-4.
19. Jeffrey P. Bezos, "2016 Letter to Shareholders," Exhibit 99.1, amazon.com entry from Securities Exchange Commission (website), https://www.sec.gov/Archives/edgar/data/1018724/000119312517120198/d373368dex991.htm.
20. Alice Hoon, Emily Oliver, Kasia Szpakowska, and Philip Newton, "Use of the 'Stop, Start, Continue' method is associated with the production of constructive qualitative feedback by students in higher education," *Assessment and Evaluation in Higher Education* 40, no. 5 (2015): 755-767.
21. Charles Duhigg, Mike Chamberlain, et al., *The Power of Habit: Why We Do What We Do in Life and Business,* illustrated ed. (Random House, 2012).
22. Melanie Chisholm, Geri Halliwell, Victoria Beckham, Emma Bunton, Melanie Brown, Matthew Paul Rowbottom, and Richard Stannar, "Wannabe," Performed by Spice Girls on their debut album *Spice,* (Sony/ATV Music Publishing LLC, Universal Music Publishing Group, Peermusic Publishing, 1996).
23. Mark Victor Hansen, "Mark Victor Hansen Wise Sayings and Quotes," Wise Sayings (website), https://www.wisesayings.com/authors/mark-victor-hansen-quotes/.
24. Zig Ziglar, *Biscuits, Fleas, and Pump Handles*, (Update, a division of Crescendo Publications Inc., 1974): 171.
25. Lund University, "New research shows that we control our forgetfulness," ScienceDaily (website), July 25, 2011, www.sciencedaily.com/releases/2011/07/110705091115.htm.

26. Russell D. Fernald, "How does behavior change the brain? Multiple methods to answer old questions," *Integrative and Comparative Biology* 43, no. 6 (2003): 771-779.

27. Yi-Yuan Tang, Changhao Jiang, and Rongxiang Tang, "How mind-body practice works—integration or separation?," *Frontiers in Psychology* 8 (2017): 866.

28. Bart Massi and Christopher H. Donahue, "Aren't sure? Brain is primed for learning," *Yale News* online, Yale University, July 19, 2018, https://news.yale.edu/2018/07/19/arent-sure-brain-primed-learning.

29. Zakary L. Tormala and Richard E. Petty, "What doesn't kill me makes me stronger: the effects of resisting persuasion on attitude certainty," *Journal of Personality and Social Psychology* 83, no. 6 (2002): 1298.

30. John Seely Brown, *Seeing Differently: Insights on Innovation* (Boston: Harvard Business Press, 1997): 245.

31. Michael N. Cline, from his personal journal dated January 2018.

**CHAPTER 8 — RESOLVING CONFLICT**

1. Eliyahu M. Goldratt is the author of the Theory of Constraints (TOC) and the TOC Thinking Process. Much of his work has influenced this chapter of the book.

2. Eliyahu M. Goldratt, *Beyond the Goal*, unabridged ed. (Gildan Media, 2011).

3. Mao Tse-tung, "Volume 1, On Contradiction," *Selected works of Mao Tse-Tung*, (August 1937).

4. A speech by HRH The Prince of Wales, "Islam and the West," given at the Oxford Centre for Islamic Studies, The Sheldonian Theatre, Oxford, 27 Oct. 1993.

5. Nathalie Gesell, Frank Niklas, Sandra Schmiedeler, and Robin Segerer, "Mindfulness and romantic relationship outcomes: The mediating role of conflict resolution styles and closeness," *Mindfulness* 11, no. 10 (2020): 2314-2324.

6. John Steinbeck, *Once There Was a War*, rev. ed. (Penguin Classics, 2007).

7. F. R. Walton, *The Library of History of Diodorus Siculus, Fragments of Book XXVI*, trans. F. R. Walton in Loeb Classical Library, Vol. XI (1957).

8. Paul Dickson, *The Official Rules: 5,427 Laws, Principles, and Axioms to Help You Cope with Crises, Deadlines, Bad Luck, Rude Behavior, Red Tape, and Attacks by Inanimate Objects* (Dover Publications, 2013).

9. Interview by Trevor Amrine, "The Real Problem is in the Hearts of Men," *New York Times Magazine* (June 23, 1946): 7. (Einstein actually said: "Many persons have inquired concerning a recent message of mine that a new type of thinking is essential if mankind is to survive and move to higher levels.")

10. Eliyahu M. Goldratt, *It's Not Luck* (North River Press, 1994).
11. Marco Verweij, Timothy J. Senior, Juan F. Domínguez D., and Robert Turner, "Emotion, rationality, and decision-making: how to link affective and social neuroscience with social theory," *Frontiers in Neuroscience* 9 (2015): 332.
12. Anthony C. Fletcher, Georges A. Wagner, and Philip E. Bourne, "Ten simple rules for more objective decision-making," *PLOS Computational Biology* 16, no. 4 (2020): e1007706.
13. Josh Billings—pen name of 19th-century American humorist Henry Wheeler Shaw. He was a famous humor writer and lecturer in the United States, perhaps second only to Mark Twain, during the latter half of the 19th century.


## CHAPTER 9 — TRANSFORMATION

1. Author's personal interview with Kristy, June 6, 2020. Named changed by mutual agreement.
2. David McCullough, *1776,* (New York: Simon & Schuster, 2005).
3. Ibid.
4. Mahatma Gandhi, "General Knowledge About Health XXXII: Accidents Snake-Bite," *The Collected Works of Mahatma Gandhi, Volume XII* (April 1913 to December 1914) (Ahmedabad, India: Navajivan Trust [Publications Division, Ministry of Information & Broadcasting, Government of India], 1964).


## ACKNOWLEDGMENTS

1. H.W. Turnbull, ed., *The Correspondence of Isaac Newton: 1661-1675, Vol 1* (London, UK: Published for the Royal Society at the University Press, 1959): 416.
2. Mosiah 3:19, *The Book of Mormon,* rev. ed. (United States of America: Intellectual Reserve, Inc., 1981).

Made in the USA
Columbia, SC
01 December 2024

47186232R00139